The Special Relationship

The Special Relationship

Anglo-American Relations and Western European Unity 1947-56

R.B. Manderson-Jones

Distributed in the United States by
CRANE, RUSSAK & COMPANY, INC.
52 Vanderbilt Avenue
New York, New York 10017

The London School of Economics and Political Science

Crane, Russak & Company, New York

Published in the United States by
Crane, Russak & Company, Inc.
52 Vanderbilt Avenue
New York, N.Y. 10017

Library of Congress Catalog Card Number 72-80106
ISBN -0-8448-0018-X
Printed in Great Britain

Contents

Contents

Preface

This book is an analysis of Anglo-American relations in the context of Western European unity from 1947 to 1956. It has been written against the background of the Cold War, the crystallisation of the United States policy of containment, and the evolution of Britain's long-term conception of her postwar role. The book is not intended to be a history but rather an analytical account of the interplay between American and British policy during the most crucial stages of progress towards European unity. This is accordingly reflected in the structure of presentation.

The study was undertaken as a doctoral thesis at the London School of Economics and Political Science, University of London. In the choice of subject my primary interest was in the undercurrent of conflict between the United States and Britain over the future of Western Europe. This divergence was centred on the degree of unity to which postwar Western Europe should aspire and on the nature of Britain's postwar role in relation to Western Europe. Although since the first British application for membership in the European Economic Community there has been near exhaustive discussion of these issues, little recognition has been given to the fact that the problem of Britain's role in Western Europe has been rooted in Anglo-American relations from the end of the Second World War. It is too commonly assumed in existing literature that Britain's opposition to participation in efforts towards European unity stemmed simply from a desire to preserve her sovereignty and to maintain her traditional world role. What is more important is that Ernest Bevin, as Foreign Secretary in the British Labour Government after the war, was pursuing a definite policy towards an inter-governmental union of Western Europe under British leadership, as a means of re-establishing Western Europe's central position in international affairs, and in particular, as a means of providing an indispensable pillar for assuring

Britain's postwar status as a first-class power. His attitude was therefore not simply opposition to European unity, but opposition to European unity as an obstacle to his own design for postwar Western Europe. Under the succeeding Conservative governments British policy was of much the same bent though not as rigorously or successfully pursued. The attitude remained one of viewing European unity as the elimination of British influence within Western Europe, and inter-governmental cooperation as strengthening it. So while the United States was seeking to 'rule' through unity, Britain was seeking to 'rule' through cooperation short of unity.

An essential element in the development of both United States and British policy was the differing degrees of importance which each attached at different times to the so-called Anglo-American 'special' relationship. On the one hand, Britain consistently throughout this period regarded the Anglo-American relationship as the mainstay of her own postwar security and that of Western Europe. On the other hand, American attitudes were quite ambivalent, viewing Britain sometimes as no more than part of Western Europe on equal footing with the continental countries; and at other times as separate from Western Europe, either as 'special' partner of the United States, or simply as a convenient bridge to Western Europe and instrument for American policies there. Thus the changing nature of the Anglo-American relationship emerges as a central theme beneath the issue of the extent of Britain's involvement in Western Europe in the fields of political, economic, and military integration, from the Marshall Plan to the creation of Western European Union (WEU).

I must record my sincere gratitude to my post-graduate supervisor Professor Geoffrey Goodwin of the London School of Economics without whose encouragement and patient advice I might never have undertaken this task.

I wish also to acknowledge my indebtedness to the many persons who kindly allowed me to impinge upon their hard-pressed time for interviews which have been of great value. My appreciation also goes out to the trustees of the various collections of private papers which were of inestimable value to my work; and to the authors and publishers whose work I have drawn upon and referred to in the text. The study was made possible by the Jamaica Independence Postgraduate Scholarship 1965, and by an award from the Central Research Fund of the University of London towards that part of the research carried out in the United States.

Genesis of American postwar attitudes: collaboration, containment, and the Marshall Plan

Following upon the Second World War, new ideas and concepts, weapons and strategies, were taking shape within an international system in which the balance of power had shifted dramatically not only in situation from the European centre, but also in the factor of power itself with the emergence of two 'super-powers'—the United States and the Soviet Union. The course of international events over the next two decades was to be largely dominated by the confrontation between the super-powers and the hardening of the East-West ideological rift. This was particularly the case in respect of events in Europe, which from the outset was the greatest stake in the Cold War, and it was accordingly inevitable that the evolution of American postwar attitudes towards Britain's relations with Western Europe, as well as towards the Western European countries themselves, would be directly influenced by American Cold War policies.

The overall reference of American Cold War policies was the idea of containment. As a strategy, containment was essentially a matter of preventing the expansion of the Soviet Union and of the communist ideology and influence; as a concept, it came to be interpreted in policy to mean American system-building within the non-communist world towards a formidable 'Western bloc'; as a philosophy, it meant coexistence with the Soviet Union until such time as the Soviet Union succumbed to internal collapse or until the Western bloc was able to bring this about. American attitudes towards future relations with the Soviet Union were far from being clear at the end of the war, and the crystallisation of containment from 1947 followed upon two short-lived approaches in dealing with the Soviet Union. Immediate postwar attempts at genuine collaboration with the Soviet Union had been set in train by Franklin D. Roosevelt. But, increasingly before his death in April 1945, President Roosevelt's efforts towards an accommodation with Russia for future cooperation in the postwar world, particularly within the framework of the United Nations, were constantly being threatened by a strong undercurrent of American criticism of 'appeasement', or of being 'too soft on the Reds'. Roosevelt died in office at a critical moment in world history, and Truman, elevated from the Vice-Presidency as his constitutional successor, was himself acutely sensitive to the unfavourable criticisms of Roosevelt's policies, and determined from the start to avoid having the stigma of 'appeasement' attached to his own. It was soon apparent that his Administration was going to be far less conciliatory in attitude towards Russia, and Truman himself confides that, on becoming President, he had the consensus of his chief military and diplomatic advisers that American agreements with the Soviet Union 'had so far been a one-way street and that this could not continue'.[1] Indeed, George Kennan, who as head of Truman's Policy Planning Staff within the State Department was responsible for the theoretical refinement of containment, admits in his *Memoirs* that even before Yalta he was himself fully opposed to 'the unrealism that prevailed in the entire approach of FDR to the problems of Eastern Europe'.[2] Nevertheless, although Truman immediately departed from his predecessor's compromising approach towards the Soviet Union, the real shift in American policy towards overt confrontation and containment did not occur for two years from Truman's succession. In this prelude to containment the Truman Administration outwardly continued the collaborative policy of Roosevelt in the various Tripartite and Four Power conferences between 1945 and 1947. But Truman's brand of 'collaboration' differed in kind from Roosevelt's and was in fact a collaboration which, based on certain fundamental miscalculations, aimed at bringing about through negotiations a Soviet capitulation to American terms of a postwar settlement, which in effect would have reversed the Soviet foothold in Germany and Eastern Europe.

The immediate concerns of Truman's Presidency were to undo the effects of the Yalta Agreement of February 1945, which had led to Soviet entrenchment in Eastern Europe during the final stages of the war, and to secure the future of Germany from any real degree of Soviet influence or control, as well as halting 'the march of Communism' in the Far and Middle East and in the Mediterranean. The Yalta Agreement stood in the postwar years as the greatest symbol of 'appeasement' to Russia. It was widely regretted as a 'sell-out' to Russia of the liberties and democratic forms of the peoples of Eastern Europe, the preservation of which was accepted as being a primary *casus belli* in the Second World War. Moreover, the vision of the Soviet Union taking firm roots in Eastern Europe entailed the nightmare possibility of Soviet penetration, forcibly or otherwise, into Western Europe with the eventual subordination of the entire continent to Communism. Certainly, few were inclined to wager that the Soviet Union's appetite for expansion would be sated before the frontiers of Western Europe; and most were only too prone to see Russia having the most aggressive intentions towards her European neighbours.

'Collaboration' as a means of coercion had a dual advantage. The Truman Administration could posture as continuing in search of a genuine peace and as being willing to work out a postwar settlement with the Soviet Union. At the same time, the Soviet Union was always in a position to be subjected to the most scathing international propaganda condemning her as obstructive to the peace, whenever she resisted, as she was bound to, Anglo-American and French pressures in the Great Power councils for a settlement which would effectively reverse the postwar European balance against her interest. But it was not merely the censorship of a large body of misguided international opinion to which the Truman Administration looked as a pressure for Russian acquiescence in American terms of a postwar settlement. President Truman's diplomacy, although privately recognising the inability to employ force to that end, invariably wore the sabre-rattling threat of force in its 'iron fist and strong language'—which was also calculated to be of domestic appeal in showing Truman to be no 'appeaser' or 'fellow traveller', as his predecessor was sometimes suspected of being.[3]

The fundamental miscalculation of the Truman Administration was the expectation that severe postwar economic prostration of Russia would make it impossible for Russia to maintain indefinitely a burdensome military presence in Europe, and would in the short run force a capitulation to American terms. Economic pressures on Russia were greatly intensified by the abrupt termination of American Lend-Lease, on 21 August 1945, and by the cancellation of plans made under Roosevelt, in late 1944, to offer Russia in the immediate post-hostilities period a large-scale loan of $3·5 billion, which Russian leaders had been led to believe that they would receive.[4] Although the full effects of the termination of

Lend-Lease were partly offset by UNRRA aid,[5] of which the
United States was the main contributor, the Truman Administration was determined to close this last source of assistance to
Russia. From the summer of 1945 efforts in this direction were
evidenced in the Administration's acceptance of George Kennan's
argument, maintained with the support of the United States
Ambassador to Russia, Averell Harriman, that there was no
'justification, either economic or political, for any further granting
of Lend-Lease aid to Russia, for any agreement on our part that
Russia, not being a contributor to UNRRA, should receive any
substantial amount of UNRRA aid, or for any extension of US
government credit to Russia without equivalent political advantage
to our people'.[6] It was clear that what was being aimed at from
that time was a complete economic boycott of Russia, and a
severing of all sources of economic assistance in order to bring
the Kremlin to its knees. When, at the end of 1946, the UNRRA
was finally terminated, this was, according to F. S. Northedge, due
to 'the feeling in Congress that UNRRA was being used to sustain
régimes unfriendly towards the United States, together with the
American taxpayer's wish to employ relief with more discrimination....'[7]

It is against this background of expecting and working for
Russian postwar economic collapse with consequent acquiescence
in an American postwar settlement, together with the immediate
American preoccupation with defeating the Japanese and the need
for Russian support there, that the real nature of the Potsdam
Agreement in August 1945 emerges. Potsdam was hardly the
'confused and unreal discussions'[8] which Kennan, for instance,
has attempted to dispose of it as. The essence of the Potsdam
Agreement lay in the zonal division of Germany among four
occupying powers, and in the decision on Four Power Agreement
and control over the future of Germany. Viewed simply in its
literary terms and with the advantage of hindsight, it might well
appear unreal. But viewed in terms of the Truman Administration's
approach to collaboration, and the Administration's prognostications on a Russian capitulation, the Potsdam Agreement can be
defended as a pragmatic *ad interim* approach to Germany. Not
only did it define and legitimise the future of Germany within the
terms of democracy, but by its zonal divisions it provided a basis
for the beginning of the economic reconstruction of at least Western
Germany on which the recovery of Western Europe as a whole

was seen to depend, while the formula of Four Power Agreement was privately interpreted to mean Anglo-American agreement in which France and Russia, in the circumstances expected at the time, would sooner than later have to acquiesce. Indeed, had the Truman Administration's calculations about Russian prostration and early Western European recovery come true, history would have been far less critical of Potsdam. The problem from the American standpoint lay not so much in the agreement but in the grave miscalculations behind the agreement and in the general pretence at collaboration. This pretence was to continue until the spring of 1947 when it was all too evident that the assumptions upon which collaboration had been based were wholly unfounded.

Four Power Agreement got off to a very bad start with the breakdown of the London Conference of Foreign Ministers in December 1945. In January 1946, although President Truman was already 'tired of babying the Soviets',[9] collaboration continued as a result of the undertaking given by Secretary of State James F. Byrnes, at the London Conference in December, to further negotiations with the Soviet Union on the minor ex-enemy peace treaties. This commitment was against President Truman's wishes, and the result was Truman's decision to dismiss Byrnes and to replace him with General George C. Marshall.[10] The decision, though taken in January 1946, could not be implemented until the beginning of 1947, following the return of General Marshall from his one-year China Mission to bolster Chiang Kai-shek. Since Byrnes had initiated the negotiations he was allowed to see them through, but Truman in 1946 was dealing with a Secretary of State in whom he no longer reposed any confidence. The minor peace treaties were finally completed and signed in October 1946, and the ground was cleared for the shift to take place in the next six months towards the policy of containment.

In the autumn of 1946, Truman, paving the way for the Marshall Plan, was 'looking for some method that would encourage the peoples of Europe to embark upon a joint undertaking eventually leading to effective self-help', and the State-War-Navy Co-ordinating Committee (SWNCC) was detailed to 'study and submit recommendations for action'.[11] It was already becoming apparent that mere emergency relief measures — through UNRRA (until the end of 1946), the Export-Import Bank, various short-term stopgap devices to soften the impact of the termination of Lend-Lease, and even the Anglo-American Financial Agreements of December 1945

—were quite inadequate for ensuring rapid transition to recovery in Western Europe. It was also recognised that Western European recovery increasingly necessitated the economic reconstruction of Germany, which was its industrial heartland. Some progress was made in this direction with the decision on 2 December 1946 to fuse the American and British zones into Bizonia. But the recovery of the full productivity of the western industrial zones of Germany necessarily depended on the support of the Russian agrarian zone, and Anglo-American efforts to have Germany treated as a single economic unit were constantly frustrated not just by the Russians but by the French as well, and were finally flatly rejected at the Moscow Conference of Foreign Ministers in March-April 1947. Economic recovery in Western Europe suffered another critical set-back by the excessively severe winter of 1946–7, which left Western Europe on the brink of complete economic collapse.

In the spring of 1947, then, not only was Western Europe facing economic disaster, but the Soviet Union, having held its own at the conference tables throughout 1945 and 1946, still showed no signs of any erosion of its foothold in Eastern Europe, and all indications were rather of its firm consolidation there. At the same time, there was the increasing spread of Communism beyond Europe. The year 1947 had begun with the failure of American efforts to forge a coalition government in China between the retreating forces of Chiang Kai-shek and the Chinese Communists, which Truman had recognised as the 'only' means of bolstering the increasingly unpopular régime of the Generalissimo.[12] Communism was also on the march in the Mediterranean, and a crisis broke over Washington when on 21 February 1947 Britain finally notified the United States of her inability to continue propping up Greece and Turkey with military and economic assistance beyond the end of March. The British announcement created grave apprehensions within the Truman Administration over the prospect of 'the extension of the Iron Curtain across the Eastern Mediterranean' with 'the clearest implications in the Middle East and Italy, Germany, and France'.[13]

These were the circumstances against which President Truman delivered his historic address to Congress on 12 March 1947, enunciating the Truman Doctrine. Although delivered in the name of a 'Special Message to Congress on Greece and Turkey', the Truman Doctrine was intended to be a statement of general policy. According to its author, the Truman Doctrine was 'America's answer to the surge of expansion of Communist tyranny', and 'the turning point in America's foreign policy, which now declared that whatever aggression, direct or indirect, threatened the peace, the security of the United States was involved'.[14] The growing conceptual division of the world into East and West was legitimised in the Truman Doctrine, where, in the words of Truman himself, 'the line had been drawn sharply'.[15] Above all, in departing from the earlier policy of trying to dislodge the Soviet Union from Eastern Europe, and in implicitly partitioning the world at the Iron Curtain,[16] President Truman left no doubt about the self-appointed role of the United States as leader of the 'free-world'[17] and committed the United States to a strategy of global containment of Communism.[18]

The first task of the United States in the spring of 1947 was to avert the impending economic catastrophe in Western Europe, and to prevent those countries from succumbing either to external communist pressures from Russia or to their rising internal communist parties by reconstructing Western Europe as a strong, successfully functioning economic and political system. In this connection the Marshall Plan, which followed in the wake of the Truman Doctrine, was not simply a shift from the earlier piecemeal transitional approach to national recovery in Western Europe, to a long-term programme of economic reconstruction based on massive dollar aid: it also signified a fundamental departure from American postwar planning for world-wide multilateralism through the Bretton Woods institutions to Western European regionalism.[19] Conceived primarily in relation to Western Europe, the formulation of the Marshall Plan rested on three basic positions. The first was that the problems of the Western European countries were inseparable, and that the best approach to their permanent solution lay in regional cooperation and integration. National reconstruction of Western Europe was thus placed firmly within the context of regional recovery, and it was basically on this account that the terms of the Marshall Plan called for a 'joint approach' to Europe. The second position was that American sponsorship of a massive European Recovery Programme should not exclude the Eastern European countries under Soviet influence if those countries were willing to participate within the wider framework of European regionalism, and were in so doing prepared 'to abandon the exclusive orientation of their economies'. The United States held out some hope that the attraction of large-scale American aid would prove irresistible, and would draw the Eastern European countries out of the Soviet orbit into a pro-American European regional scheme; or failing that, it would at least provoke some disaffection within the Eastern camp if Eastern European interests in accepting the Marshall Plan were thwarted by Russia. The third position was in relation to Russia. The United States would naturally have preferred to exclude Russia from the scope of the Marshall offer. There was the fear of possible Russian sabotage of the Marshall Plan by an acceptance of the offer accompanied by a refusal to participate on terms acceptable to the United States. This itself, by forcing the United States into the position of having to renege on its original offer in order to surmount the possibility of Russian sabotage of Western European recovery, could be further exploited by Russia as an indication of the underlying dominative imperialist intentions of American assistance to Europe. Against this, however, it was fairly obvious that if Russia was from the start excluded from the Marshall Plan offer it could still pursue the self-same argument, and indeed with greater credibility since it would not then be in the position to be accused of attempted sabotage. Moreover, could the Marshall Plan reasonably be open in scope to Eastern Europe while excluding Russia, or would not the Eastern European countries be more prone to come out openly in favour of the Plan if it did not exclude Russian participation from the outset? In any case even if the offer were left open to Russia, what was the real likelihood of Russian acceptance? Might not the Russian response be prompt denouncement of the Marshall Plan, thus providing the United States with the opportunity of proceeding without Russia while avoiding the accusation of not having extended the offer to her? The Truman Administration clearly recognised a tactical propaganda advantage in leaving the option of participation open to Russia, for while the Administration considered it unlikely that Russia could ever agree to participate in a joint European Recovery Programme, a rejection of the Marshall Plan on the part of Russia would enable the Truman Administration and its successors for ever to assert that Russia and not the United States had been responsible for the final division of postwar Europe. Altogether the balance of the arguments appeared, therefore, to hang in favour of extending the Marshall offer to Russia, or at least not excluding Russia from its scope. For there was after all another alternative, and it was precisely this which was eventually followed: that is, the safest path of simply extending the Marshall offer vaguely to Europe 'as a whole', indicating neither exclusion nor inclusion of Russia or any other country by name.

The immediate reaction to Secretary of State Marshall's celebrated Harvard Address of 5 June 1947 came from British Foreign Secretary, Ernest Bevin. It was clear that Britain was expected to take the lead in organising a joint European response as Bevin had received information regarding the seriousness of the Harvard Address[20] which was a real tactical advantage in view of its frankly unceremonious 'matter-of-fact' manner of delivery.[21] Bevin immediately initiated discussions in Paris on 17 and 18 June with the French Foreign Minister, Georges Bidault, aimed at establishing an Anglo-French position towards Russian participation.[22] Between the Bevin-Bidault discussions and their preliminary conference on the Marshall Plan with the Russian Foreign Minister, Molotov, from 27 June to 3 July, there were informal Anglo-American talks in London, from 22 to 25 June, among Assistant Secretary of State for Economic Affairs William Clayton, United States Ambassador Lewis Douglas, Prime Minister Attlee, Bevin, the Chancellor of the Exchequer, Hugh Dalton, and, shortly to be his successor, Sir Stafford Cripps. In these talks the British were briefed in detail on American thinking behind the Marshall Plan, and it was understood:

> that while it is hoped the scheme will cover Europe as a whole, *the US Administration would be satisfied if it could be started with the Western Countries of Europe as a nucleus,* on the understanding that the scheme is to be open to other countries if they so desired.[23]

At the tripartite conference between Foreign Ministers Bevin, Bidault, and Molotov, the Russian representative was greeted with a prior Anglo-French decision to convene a strictly European conference for the collective assessment of the requirements of a joint European recovery programme. According to Truman, Bevin and Bidault 'proposed to lay out the agenda and procedure for the plenary meeting of the conference'.[24] The inference in any case was clear enough—the Russians would either have to accede to the Anglo-French proposals or withdraw, or be accused of blocking progress.[25] On 2 July the Russians withdrew from the preliminary conference on the Marshall Plan, with the explanation that the nature of the Marshall proposal 'would inevitably result in the

B

imposition of the will of the stronger European Powers upon other European countries'.[26] The Russians had sought a statement in figures of the proposed American aid scheme,[27] and their preference was for direct allocations to individual countries according to their needs as individually assessed by them, and without any scrutiny of one another's affairs or control over the use of the aid.[28] They withdrew as soon as it became apparent that their approach had been effectively blocked by prior Anglo-French agreement on procedure,[29] and that the alternative would involve a growth of economic ties between the Eastern European countries and the West, with unacceptable consequences for Russia herself and for her foothold in those countries.[30]

The significance of the Russian withdrawal from the preliminary conference on the Marshall Plan has been greatly inflated by those who would seek to attribute to it the origin of the Cold War.[31] Of far more significance are the reasons for extending the offer to Russia in the first place. In this connection it must be recalled that Marshall's conviction, on his return from the Moscow Conference, was that 'the idea of approaching the solution of Europe's problem in collaboration with the Russians was a pipe dream',[32] and this view was shared by the entire Administration and the Planning Staff.[33] To the extent that 'the door was left open' (much in the manner of an entrance leading directly to an exit) it was therefore partly a façade—Marshall held that 'if Europe was to be divided he was not going to be the person to divide it'.[34] Yet this was a patently false position in three respects. Firstly, it was totally inconsistent with the actual formulation of the Marshall Plan, which was conceived primarily in relation to Western Europe[35] with an implicit recognition of the reality of a division in Europe, already acknowledged in the Truman Doctrine. Secondly, it would have been idle to expect that the Marshall Plan, conceived as it was to provide the Western European nations with 'a realistic argument against the Communists' counsel of despair',[36] and whose conception was not that of charitable relief but of politico-economic necessity[37] directed to the reconstruction of capitalism, would be acceptable to Russia. In fact, it was neither intended nor expected that Russia would participate in the Marshall Plan,[38] and indeed the Administration was quite surprised by Russia's apparent interest,[39] although Truman confesses only to being 'a little' surprised.[40] In the third place, in so far as the Administration would have welcomed it if the Eastern European countries found themselves sufficiently tempted by the Marshall offer to defect from the Soviet orbit, this itself was not only evidence of their acknowledgement of a division of Europe but testimony to their intention to try to separate the Eastern European states from Russia.

Following the withdrawal of Russia, Britain and France called a conference in Paris on July 12 for consideration of a joint approach to European recovery. All the European countries except Spain were invited but the conference was not attended by the Eastern European countries, including Czechoslovakia, all of which followed Russia's edict and decided against cooperation in an American-sponsored European recovery programme. The outcome of the conference was the creation of the Committee for European Economic Cooperation (CEEC), which was assigned the task of framing a report assessing the overall requirements of European reconstruction. In September 1947 the CEEC's report was completed and its findings were sent to the United States. In passing the Economic Cooperation Act (April) 1948, Congress reduced the figure recommended by the Administration, on the basis of its own analysis of the CEEC's report, and gave authority only for annual appropriations for European recovery, instead of accepting the Administration's suggestion for an overall allocation for a four-year programme. It was clear even from this stage that Congress not only intended to maintain full control over the amount, nature, and utilisation of American aid for European recovery, but wanted to ensure that further appropriations were made only on the basis of satisfactory progress towards European recovery within a regional integrationist framework. For this reason, the legislation established the Economic Cooperation Administration (ECA) as an independent agency for the administration of American aid, with separate missions to the recipient countries. President Truman's first choice for the position of ECA Chief Administrator had been Dean Acheson. But Truman subsequently decided on Paul G. Hoffman, a Republican supporter and President of Studebaker Corporation, after he had been confidentially informed by Senator A. H. Vandenberg, the Republican leader in the Republican-controlled 80th Congress, that 'the Senate and the country was assured that the Administrator would be a big industrialist' and that the nomination of Acheson would certainly be rejected.[41] Hoffman himself proved a determined integrationist, with enough influence and latitude to take full initiative from the Administration in implementing the European Recovery Programme. As a direct link between the ECA and the Organisation for European Economic Cooperation (OEEC), into which the CEEC had transformed itself on 16 April 1948, and which was the European organisation responsible for the execution of the four-year programme, the Truman Administration created the post of United States Special Representative in Europe, filled by Ambassador W. Averell Harriman.[42]

The European Recovery Programme was launched in April 1948[43] and immediately became the main focus of the Administration for Western European economic integration. The regional integrationist approach to recovery had, of course, been central to the Marshall Plan, and was consistently advocated in all the background reports of the Special (*ad hoc*) Committee (SWNCC), the Committee on Extension of Aid to Foreign Governments, in the Clayton Memorandum, and the Kennan Policy Planning Staff papers.[44] Despite discreet avoidance of the term in the Harvard Address, integration was still very much behind Secretary Marshall's stipulation of a joint European programme.[45] In 1947 there were compelling economic arguments in support of integration for permanently overcoming 'excessive fragmentation, the lack of competitive flexibility in commercial exchanges, the lack, in particular, of a large consumer's market'.[46] Strengthened as these were by undisguised American interest in the last possibility, there were also significant political considerations; the framework integration would provide for reconstituting Western Germany, for example, while generally increasing political stability within Western Europe by providing a *cordon sanitaire* against Communism and a foundation for eventual Western European unity. American interest in Western European unity was essentially an expression of the American postwar confrontation with the Soviet Union. To view it as a mere reflection of the common predisposition of Americans to apply their own eighteenth-century constitutional solutions to Western Europe is to grossly oversimplify the situation, and to overlook the grave American suspicions of a general 'ganging up' which were always attendant on the occasional pronouncements for European unity coming from a handful of influential Continental figures during the inter-war years. The shift in the postwar era to a position of active American encouragement of the idea of Western European unity was a transformation arising from the profound apprehension of the threat posed by the Soviet Union and the Communist ideology to the civilisation of the North Atlantic. Heightened by victory, the passionate emotional rationalisation of the Second World War as a struggle between the forces of good and evil was transferred to the Cold War in the context of a struggle to preserve Western civilisation against Communism. The universalist conception of confrontation was interpreted in the American policy of containment to involve a course of Western system-building as a counterpoise to the increasingly monolithic structure of the Soviet Union. In this context the idea of European unity took on a new and special meaning. The significance of Western European unity went beyond the means it would provide for the ending of European national rivalries which twice in but two and half decades had brought the world to war, and transcended the economic solution it would offer for Europe's ills through a recognition of the relationship between postwar economic viability and regional integration. Its ultimate significance lay in the American desire to create a formidable Western bloc around a North Atlantic system, comprising a strong united Western Europe, on the one hand, and North America (the United States and Canada), on the other; and American foreign policy from 1947, in switching dramatically from the Rooseveltian premise of world-wide multilateralism and the global internationalism of the United Nations, embraced Western European regionalism as the path towards economic and eventual political unity of Western Europe, as a pillar of the Western system.

Following upon the Truman Doctrine, Congressional clamour for European unity began with a resolution on 21 March 1947, sponsored by Senators J. W. Fulbright and E. D. Thomas and Representative Boggs, favouring 'the creation of a United States of Europe', towards which Secretary Marshall, on the eve of his Harvard Address, found himself 'deeply sympathetic'.[47] In November 1947 John Foster Dulles, who had been publicly advocating European unification from January of that year, recommended to Congress that the Marshall Plan be used as 'a positive instrument for a United Western Europe',[48] while at the level of informed public opinion Walter Lippmann was ardently advocating 'no less than economic union' for Europe. With the launching of the European Recovery Programme, American enthusiasm was soon evidenced in legislation, notably in the (1950) amendment to the Economic Cooperation Act of 1948, which added: 'It is further declared to be the policy of the people of the United States to encourage the unification of Europe'.[49]

Despite the various pronouncements for European unity, there were between 1947 and 1950 wide divergences between the Administration and radical elements in Congress over such issues as the area to be covered, the most suitable organisational and constitutional forms, and, above all, the real priority of European unity in American policy. The radical 'Europeanists' in Congress[50] considered European unity as the first call on United States foreign policy in Western Europe. They saw political unity as the prerequisite to permanent economic recovery and supported frequent suggestions that American aid be made contingent on concrete progress towards political unity. The Truman Administration, however, tended to view European unity as a long-term objective — something which could only emerge from 'the deep feeling of the European peoples themselves and [could] not be improvised'.[51] As Secretary of State, and aware that constant pressure for European unity might well be counter-productive, Acheson held that the Europeans had it as 'their right to decide democratically, as our founding fathers did, when, how and whether they will federate'.[52] The immediate priority of the Administration was with European economic recovery as a means of consolidating the region against Communism and, through integration, as the pre-condition for ultimate unity. '... [I]mmediate union', argued Deputy ECA Administrator Howard Bruce, 'would necessarily result in serious maladjustments and retard the overall Western European recovery ... the economic recovery which is being made possible by Marshall Plan aid is the most important factor readying Europe for actual economic and political union; to make such aid contingent on political union would be to put the cart before the horse....'[53] No European policy was laid down in hard and fast lines, and until the supranational stage of the European movement, commencing with the Schuman Plan of May 1950, the Truman Administration hoped for progress towards European unity through significant developments in intra-European cooperation and gradual integration within the economic and military spheres — the OEEC and the Brussels Treaty Organisation — in conjunction with the growth of the Council of Europe. Some of the ardent 'Europeanists' in Congress, led by Senator J. W. Fulbright, disputed what they considered a too rigid separation by the Administration of its economic, military and political

approaches to Western Europe, and Senator Fulbright even feared
that the ECA's exclusively economic purpose was actually aiding
the revival of European prewar nationalism in so far as the
national economies were being rebuilt without a framework of
poitical unity.[54] Nevertheless the Administration itself was
cautious and in the pressing circumstances of the time preferred
to lay the foundation of Western European unity by concentrating
on the immediate ends of Western European recovery and
economic integration. Above all the Truman Administration
awaited far-reaching initiatives from Western Europe, and looked
in particular to Britain as the natural leader of the postwar
European movement.

2

Conflicting designs and American ambivalencies concerning Britain's postwar role

From Marshall's Harvard Address to Britain's refusal in June 1950 to participate in the negotiations on the Schuman Plan, the United States continuously looked to Britain for leadership of the postwar Western European movement. In the formulation of the Marshall Plan there had been some general debate on the question of the inclusion of Britain. But the wider issue of Britain's future relations with Western Europe, in the light of her traditional world role and the evolving long-term conception of American policy, never in fact received the kind of consideration which it warranted in the formative period of American postwar policy. On the whole, the Administration seemed simply to assume that Britain, having relinquished the seat of world leadership to the United States, would gradually fit into its European schemes. In framing the Marshall Plan, the Policy Planning Staff's Paper of 23 May 1947 distinguished between the position of Britain and that of the continental European countries, recommending separate consideration of Britain: 'The overall European programme must embrace, or be linked to, some sort of plan for dealing with the economic plight of Britain. The plan must be formally a British one, worked out on British initiative and responsibility, and the role of the United States, again, must be to give friendly support.'[1] This recommendation is of some significance in the long undercurrent of controversy within the United States over Britain's postwar role. George Kennan, who refers to himself in his *Memoirs* as an 'Anglo-American', was firmly opposed to the inclusion of Britain alongside the continental countries in a general European recovery programme. The Planning Staff subscribed to his view that the most desirable postwar evolution would be the development of a continental European unity, on the one hand, linked across the Atlantic to a close US–UK–Canadian maritime trading bloc, on the other hand.[2]

The Planning Staff's proposal was not, however, given any serious consideration by the Administration. The Administration's immediate preoccupation was devising a comprehensive economic recovery programme for Western Europe. Apart from its recognition of the virtual impossibility of an anti-British Republican Congress considering further separate treatment for Britain, if indeed Congress even passed the ERP, the Administration tended to see Britain as an integral part of postwar Western Europe. Unlike Kennan, who assumed that 'the driving force behind any movement towards political unification on the Continent, and the dominant influence within any federal union that came into being, would be, naturally and unquestionably, France',[3] the Administration recognised the indispensability of the British economy to any meaningful regional integration. Moreover it was felt that progress towards eventual European unity necessarily depended on Britain, since France, the only alternative leader, was not only too weak and unstable but contained very influential communist elements. Britain on the other hand, although considerably weakened, survived as a power in Western Europe after the ravages of the war, and Britain alone in that respect seemed able to provide the political impetus and moral revival for Western European recovery. Above all, and central to the United States recognition of Britain's special importance in the European movement, was the historical Anglo-American relationship which, coupled with Britain's traditional influence on the continent, made Britain appear a natural bridge for American policies in Europe.

The Anglo-American relationship attained its zenith during the Second World War. As H. C. Allen writes,

The Second World War ... formed an altogether fitting climax in the long drama of Anglo-American friendship. It saw, in the words of General Marshall, 'the most complete unification of military effort ever achieved by two allied nations'. It saw a co-ordination between the political authorities of two sovereign states possibly unsurpassed in history. It saw a maturing of the cordiality between the two peoples more swift and complete than all but the most optimistic prophets of Anglo-American comity had hoped.[4]

In this unique alliance, however, the true extent of the transformation in the basis of the Anglo-American relationship occasioned by the Second World War was hardly foreseen. Final victory over the enemy, by removing the strongest bond in Anglo-American wartime cooperation, saw this transformation display itself in dissonant tendencies, which during the immediate post-hostilities period threatened the survival into peacetime of a 'special' Anglo-American relationship. Britain having entered the war as a first-class power and borne the brunt of it alone, was unable to accept her postwar second-class status and dependence on America, which, entering the war in its later stages, assumed the preponderant position within the alliance and emerged far richer and more powerful than before. Such a subordination in role was a severe trauma for the British, and Anglo-American relations in the postwar years largely revolved around the problem of mutual recognition of the changed positions within the Anglo-American relationship and within the international system. The process of readjustment was not assisted either by open British resentment towards the United States and feelings of being badly done by as the real victor of the war, or by the all too apparent eagerness of the United States to assert its new found primacy in the postwar world. At the end of the war there was a swift degeneration in Anglo-American relationships with the emergence of conflicts which had been effectively suppressed by the wartime effort. There was the re-appearance of old American suspicions of British imperialism, the resentment at having to pay Britain's way after the war—at having 'to pick British Chestnuts out of the Fire'—and there were the new suspicions surrounding the socialism of the British Labour Government of 1945. On the other side of the Atlantic, there was the depth of ill-feeling generated in Britain by the rapid dismantling by the United States of the structure of the wartime alliance, by the sudden termination of Lend-Lease, by the friction-ridden negotiations and the onerous terms of the Anglo-American Loan Agreement of December 1945, and by the MacMahon Act of 1946 which decidedly undermined earlier agreements for postwar Anglo-American cooperation in the nuclear field. But just as serious frictions within the wartime alliance were effectively over-shadowed by the elaborate all-embracing joint structure of collaboration, so too in the rapidly deteriorating international atmosphere from 1947 with the growing confrontation between East and West, did the need for Anglo-American cooperation come to transcend the sharp postwar differences between the two countries, and lead to a revival of the Anglo-American alliance.

Although the revival of the Anglo-American alliance largely owed itself to a mutual recognition of general interdependence in the developing East-West rift,[5] as it emerged the alliance came to be seen separately by each party as an instrument for different ends in the reshaping of the postwar world. On the part of the United States, the joint Anglo-American front which developed over Germany, and the creation of Bizonia, spelt a degree of Anglo-American cooperation which could be fashioned into an instrument for American policies in Europe. An important consideration here was that in the immediate aftermath of the war when France was often at the other extreme of American policies, especially over Germany where France was indeed far more aligned with the Soviet Union, Britain stood roughly midway between the French and American positions. The United States in these circumstances soon not only recognised the need for a close rapport with Britain, but was also aware that the development of a common Anglo-American position, as in the case of Germany, would sooner or later force France to fall into line with the other two major Western powers. In seeking to organise Western Europe, therefore, the United States tended to emphasise not only the salient factors of Britain's stability and economic-military strength relative to the grave weakness of the continental countries, but to see the growing Anglo-American front, together with British influence on the Continent, as a bridge for American policies in Western Europe. The American postwar drive for Western European economic integration and eventual unity quickly obscured the basic differences in Britain's general position in relation to the continental countries, and overlooking Britain's historical role which was centred away from Europe and on her overseas connections, Washington soon came to see the Anglo-American relationship as the axis on which the European movement would proceed, under British leadership, towards a pro-American united Western Europe.

The American view of the Anglo-American relationship was part of the process of adjustment to the postwar transformation in their respective roles, and this was psychologically considerably easier for the United States than for Britain. At the end of the war there was no question of a return to isolationism by the United States, and President Truman was not only quick to assume the mantle of postwar leadership, but in the Truman Doctrine threw down the gauntlet to the Soviet Union and international communism. In its self-appointed leadership of the 'free-world' the United States, although demonstrating inescapable ambivalencies on the score of Britain's postwar role, generally viewed Britain as a shrunken power which could no longer pursue a world role within an international system now dominated by two super-powers, and the prevailing American tendency was to relegate Britain to the task of realistically accepting in the postwar era a European destiny in the role of junior partner to the United States in its postwar system-building against communism. But Britain, on the other hand, was psychologically incapable of accepting the diminution in her power and status. Her immediate postwar dependence on the United States was seen as being only of passing significance on the way toward full national recovery in a very short time, and it was difficult for the British to avoid the feeling that centuries of experience at the centre of world politics could effectively reduce the real gap between themselves and the Americans in terms of postwar power and influence while ensuring the rule of reason within the international system. 'Bent but by no means bowed' was the British posture, and it was Britain's policy for fully a decade and a half after the war to try to bridge the balance of power between herself and the two postwar colossi. There was thus an element of insidious rivalry beneath the Anglo-American relationship, and while the United States viewed it as an instrument for American system-building, Britain, belying the postwar realities, saw it as the pillar of her own diametrically opposed design for reinstating herself as a major world power.

Until the Anglo-Soviet alliance of 1942, Britain's traditional policy towards Europe had centred on the maintenance of a continental balance of power without any direct commitment there. Following the war, as the Anglo-Soviet alliance disappeared in the widening East-West rift, and as the Soviet Union entrenched itself in Eastern Europe, the prevention of penetration by Russia into the remaining vacuum in Western Europe was the immediate concern of Britain. The automatic mechanisms of the European balance of power system had been fully destroyed with the total collapse of the continental powers as a consequence of the war. In the new situation, the Soviet Union seemed poised to realise Britain's historical nightmare of continental Europe being dominated by a single power, and Britain saw herself called upon to redress the balance. One significant result of the war was thus the acceptance by Britain of an increased European role. Britain alone could not, however, effectively restore and permanently safeguard a Western European balance against Russia. Accordingly, both the Coalition Government and its successor in 1945, the Labour Government, anxiously looked towards the United States as the guarantor of a postwar European balance. But the problem as the Labour Government saw it was not just Russia but, in a different sense, the United States as well. For although Bevin was very awake to the Russian threat he was generally optimistic about an eventual accommodation with Russia provided there was a realistic balance against her—'we shan't reach any agreement but we shall live together'[6] was his basic attitude. On the other hand, however, his concern to prevent further Russian expansion in Europe was matched by the underlying apprehension he had of precipitate tendencies in Washington which he feared could unleash another war.[7] Besides this there was the fundamental problem of trying to preserve and strengthen Britain's traditional world role in face of the need for an American guarantee of Western European security and the postwar economic dependence of Britain and the continent on the United States. For the time, the destiny of Western Europe seemed to lie in America's hands. But the American conception of a world divided into two confronting blocs with each country being pigeon-holed under United States or Russian leadership[8] jarred with British foreign policy, which had its own designs for Western Europe. This sought to maintain an independent world role for Britain through paramountcy in a loose European concert underpinned by an Anglo-American alliance through which Whitehall could effectively influence the policies of Washington. From the standpoint of security, successive British governments naturally found it to their own advantage that the enlightened self-interest of the United States was itself inextricably bound up with the fate of Western Europe. But while the United States visualised its own interests and the salvation of Western Europe being best served by Western European unity, British policy looked in quite a different direction and constantly stopped short at close inter-governmental cooperation among the Western European countries. Britain could never see the day when she would submerge her sovereignty in Europe. Opposed to European unity for herself, Britain moreover would never countenance any kind of continental unity as this would

inevitably mean the domination of Europe by a single great power,
either from within the new entity, or in terms of the control of
the entity itself over the continent, or both. Europe in short
must never be united in the supranational sense—inter-governmental union, yes, but not unity. According to Bevin:

> No one disputes the idea of European unity. That is not the issue.
> The issue is whether European unity cannot be achieved without
> the domination and control of one great power. That is the issue
> which has to be solved ... I am sure this House and the world will
> realise that if a policy is pursued by any one power to try to
> dominate Europe by whatever means, direct or indirect—one has to
> be frank—one is driven to the conclusion that it will inevitably lead
> again to another world war and I hope this idea will be discarded
> by all of us. It is this which His Majesty's Government have striven
> and will continue to strive to prevent.[9]

Under the astute leadership of Ernest Bevin, British foreign
policy between 1947 and 1950 had both a clear long-term conception of Britain's role, and, unlike American policy, a fairly
systematic direction towards it attainment. The object was a
continuing independent international role with diplomatic readjustments towards the creation of a third centre of power, strong
enough to ensure Britain a permanent seat at the summit level of
the postwar international system. The diminution of British power
relative to the United States and the Soviet Union could be
compensated for by securing British paramountcy in a closely-knit
Western European inter-governmental union linked to the Commonwealth and the British Empire. Bevin certainly did not sub-
scribe to the Third Force sentiments of the Bevanite left wing of
the Labour Government, and never shared the sympathies of some
of the continentals for a united and neutral Western Europe standing between the two colossi. Although in search of an independent
world role he always recognised the fundamental importance of
alliance with the US. But conceptually he perceived a world
divided into three spheres of influence—the Western Hemisphere,
the Soviet sphere, and what he termed 'the middle of the planet'
where Western European influence and control were paramount.[10]
The drawing together of the Western European countries and their
interests within this last sphere towards the formation of a powerful Euro-centric system, so-called Western Union, was the ultimate
conception of Bevin's foreign policy.

While Bevin's diplomacy contrived 'to organise the middle of the planet' in the hope of creating a formidable British-led Western Union at the centre of international politics, the substantive basis for this grouping was to be found in the combined utilisation of the resources of the overseas possessions and areas under the influence of the Western European states. Britain herself looked mainly to her Black African colonies, her interests in the Middle East, and to the Commonwealth. 'If we only pushed on and developed Africa', contended Bevin, 'we could have [the] US dependent on us, and eating out of our hand, in four or five years.'[11] There is no doubt that a basic element in the British design to rebuild a world role in the postwar era was the renewed and vigorous conjoint exploitation by Western Europe of the overseas territories under its influence. In this regard Britain was not slow to recognise the value of the Commonwealth concept as a framework for the imminent dissolution of Empire commencing in the postwar phase of the decolonisation process with the independence of India and Pakistan on 15 August 1947, and of Burma and Ceylon in January and February 1948, following a long period of activist nationalist movements within these countries. The revision of the Commonwealth concept to make room for the 'sovereign independent republics', the beatific vision of a multiracial Commonwealth, and the arrangement for more frequent Commonwealth conferences were significant developments in British policy. The Commonwealth was being structured to provide an important support for Britain's new postwar role within Western Union. Bevin's views on this, as reported by Hugh Dalton, are quite clear—'The United Kingdom must keep in step with the Commonwealth and it had been recently agreed that there should be two meetings a year of Commonwealth Ministers'. He hoped, continues Dalton, 'that, later on, the Commonwealth and Western Europe might grow together. This would make a really great Third Power in the world. But this could only come slowly. Meanwhile we in Western Europe must grow together. At the recent Commonwealth Conference it had been decided that Commonwealth Governments should be "kept in close touch" with all further developments of Western Union.'[12] Beneath this was not simply the view of the Commonwealth developing as an important grouping in international politics. There was the pronounced neo-imperialism of using the Commonwealth concept, free as it was of the more pernicious connotations of colonialism, to perpetuate the historical economic and political orientations towards Britain of those of her colonies which would emerge as independent states during the postwar era. Almost as if he had perceived the European Community of the Six, without its supranational element, but blessed with its modern pseudopodium of 'association', Bevin from the late forties visualised a dynamic Western European hegemonic Union over a third of the world, comprising the primary areas of European influence and control, which would be securely preserved in the postwar era, if not by open colonialism, by the perpetuation in one form or another of the historical dependence of these areas on the European centre.[13] There needed to be no friction with either the United States or Russia since each would have its share of the world while Europe commanded the 'middle of the planet'. In his address before the House of Commons, on 22 January 1948, the British Foreign Secretary laid bare the essentials of his Western Union design:

Perhaps I may now return to the subject of the organisation in respect of *a Western Union*. That is its right description. I would emphasise that I am not concerned only with Europe as a geographical conception. Europe has extended its influence throughout the world, and we have to look further afield. In the first place, we turn our eyes to Africa, where great responsibilities are shared by us with South Africa, France, Belgium and Portugal, and equally to all overseas territories, especially of South East Asia, with which the Dutch are closely concerned. *The organisation of Western Europe must be economically supported. That involves the closest possible collaboration with the Commonwealth and with overseas territories, not only British but French, Dutch, Belgian and Portuguese.*

These overseas territories are large primary producers, and their standard of life is evolving rapidly and is capable of great development. They have raw materials, food and resources which can be turned to very great common advantage, both to the people of the territories themselves, to Europe, and to the world as a whole. The *other two* great world Powers, the United States and Soviet Russia, have tremendous resources. There is no need of conflict with them in this matter at all. If Western Europe is to achieve its balance of payments and to get a world equilibrium, it is essential that those resources should be developed and made available, and the exchange between them carried out in a correct and proper manner. There is no conflict between the social and economic development of those overseas territories to the advantage of their people, and their development as a source of supplies for Western Europe, as a contributor, as I have indicated, so essential to the balance of payments. . . .

Now I want to say a word about the United States, which seems to be a sort of bogy in the minds of a good many people. ... They are a democratic country trying to look where they are going, and what responsibilities they are undertaking. Our primary task, as I have said, is to build up with our friends in Western Europe. We have to get resources together and repair a war-damaged continent, and we have to carry out the development of these new resources overseas. The United States and the countries of Latin America are clearly as much a part of our common Western civilisation as are the nations of the British Commonwealth. The power and resources of the United States—indeed, I would say the power and resources of all the countries on the continent of America—will be needed if we are to create a solid, stable and healthy world.[14]

The realisation of Bevin's long-term conception of Western Union had first of all to overcome the realities of Western European economic weakness and military insecurity in the immediate postwar years. This is where British and American policies towards Western Europe came into direct collision. Bevin fully realised that only a permanent commitment by the United States could under-pin Western European recovery and the evolution of Western Union. To the extent that the United States could be brought to guarantee the security of a reconstructed Western Europe, to that extent would the United States be the sheet-anchor for Britain's pursuit of a revised world role. The problem was that the interest of the United States was in Western European unity, not inter-governmental union, but economic integration and ultimate political unity, and even assuming that the United States could be brought permanently out of its historical isolationist tendencies to make a commitment to Western Europe, it would unquestion-ably want to attach Western European unity as a condition of commitment. The result of this reasoning was the development of a multilateral Atlanticist approach in British thinking as a counter to the European regional integrationist perspective of Washington, and its bilateral or so-called 'dumb-bell' Atlantic vision. While the Americans were pressing for Western European unity as the basis of the region's security, Bevin's argument in terms of what he chose to call the 'new paradox' was that European unity was possible only within a wider Atlantic framework: the point being that until the United States agreed to participate in an Atlantic security system European unity in any form was quite unrealistic since the Western Europeans individually or collectively had not

c

the means to ensure their security against the Russian threat. According to Bevin:

The organisation of all the Western European democracies, excellent and necessary though it is, in present circumstances can hardly be accomplished save within the framework of some even larger entity. I am not content to confine either propaganda or speeches or action to the assumption that Western Europe alone can save itself.[15]

It was on Bevin's initiative and due very much to his own personal diplomacy that the Atlanticist approach eventually took practical form in the North Atlantic Treaty Organisation. But the first step towards the Atlantic formula was a Western European association in the Brussels Treaty Organisation of 17 March 1948,[16] which was conceived with the dual purpose of providing the foundation-stone for Western Union and for drawing the United States into an Atlantic system which would underpin Western Europe. The five-power Brussels Treaty represented for Bevin a 'fresh departure in British policy'[17] and consolidated a nucleus around Britain, France, and the Benelux countries, all of which, with the exception of Luxembourg, were imperialist powers together controlling the bulk of Europe's extensive overseas interests and possessions. Such identity of interests, together with strong Anglophile sentiments in the Benelux countries, as well as France's insecurity and reliance on the British commitment in the Anglo-French Treaty of Dunkirk (4 March 1947), appeared to place Britain in the position of being able to exert considerable influence on the direction of the policies of these countries. The wings of Western Union would inevitably spread themselves, and although it was the OEEC which eventually appeared as the potential basis for a wider Western Union, Bevin in looking to the formation of the Brussels Treaty Organisation was content to secure the support of the 'inner circle of Five' before gradually moving outwards. This was the same approach when it came to questions of political arrangements for Western Europe, as in the case of the Council of Europe which he felt 'should begin with five only — United Kingdom, France and Benelux — and be prepared to add others from time to time'.[18]

The difficulty of extracting an explicit American guarantee to the defence of Western Europe was overcome by British and French insistence that European recovery and progress towards unity could not proceed in an atmosphere of military insecurity, and by the rapid deterioration in the East-West international climate from the spring of 1948. During discussions in April 1948 on the possibility of an American commitment to Western Europe, Under-Secretary of State Lovett strongly emphasised 'the fear that existed, particularly in France, but also to a considerable extent in Britain, and which frightened those countries from moving ahead vigorously along the lines laid down by the Brussels Agreement', that is towards closer economic, political and military cooperation and unity.[19] But the particular form of the American commitment, participation in the regional multilateral North Atlantic Treaty Organisation, owed much to the prior existence of the BTO and to Bevin's diplomacy, which was instrumental in leading the Truman Administration to the conviction that nothing short of a formal American treaty commitment to the Western European countries would relieve their profound insecurity, and that such a commitment should be based on a regional Atlantic concept.[20] By joining NATO, however, the United States not only found itself pursuing conflicting approaches towards Britain and Western Europe, but also that its own policies were to the advantage of Britain which was interested least of all in the kind of Western European unity which the Americans sought in their own long-term conception of a two-pillar Atlantic community.

Apart from the inherent conflict between American and British long-term conceptions of Britain's role in relation to Western Europe, there was also the immediate internal conflict within United States policy surrounding the Anglo-American relationship as an instrument of containment and the need for British leadership of the European movement towards unity. In the Truman Doctrine the United States had boldly proclaimed itself defender of the 'free world'. But whether in adopting a policy, as Truman expressed it, 'to support free peoples', or a strategy as advanced by Kennan, in the well-known 'X-Article', of 'confronting the Russians with unalterable counterforce "at every point where they show signs of encroaching upon the interests of a peaceful world" '[21] the United States was undertaking a global commitment which it alone could not fulfil.[22] To pursue a strategy of global 'containment' and to establish a sound military position in the West, it was necessary for the United States to rely heavily on Britain, as its number one ally, in the revived Anglo-American alliance. It was accepted from 1947, and even after the creation of NATO, that the primary instrument for American 'containment' over the short-run would have to be the Anglo-American alliance. Britain, the Administration well knew, was as Senator Hubert Humphrey emphasised 'the keystone to our North Atlantic defense system'.[23] The position of Britain in the Administration's thinking on defence matters was, therefore, quite distinct from continental Western Europe. As the Administration became increasingly preoccupied with defence, from 1949, and as Britain progressed towards nuclear status, so much the more did the United States tend to see Britain separately from the continental countries, and allowed the Anglo-American alliance to overshadow the question of British participation in the European movement. Moreover, besides the military importance of Britain in Western defence, there was the obvious connection between British imperialism and global 'containment' of Communism. Dulles was not alone in holding the conviction that 'the Soviet Communists always put first on their program what they call "colonial" and "dependent" areas. China, the oil of Persia and the Middle East, and colonial Africa....'[24] Truman, despite his primary concern with Europe, had acted decisively to crush the 'giant pincers movement' in the Near East and the Mediterranean,[25] and out of recognition of Britain's role in propping up the régimes in Greece and Turkey had responded dramatically with the Truman Doctrine when Britain served notice that she could no longer afford to do so. From the American standpoint, there were manifold dangers in the decolonisation process rapidly set into motion with the independence of India, Pakistan, Burma and Ceylon. Not only was Nehru's concept of non-alignment quite repugnant to the Truman Administration, and to Acheson in particular,[26] but the emergence of these states provided a new focus for Soviet influence in Asia at a time when Communism had already overrun China, was succeeding in Korea, and the Indo-China nationalist struggle was taking an adverse turn for French imperialism with every chance of Communism succeeding there also. In such circumstances, the convenience to the United States of the forms of British imperialism—Commonwealth and empire—in yoking the peoples and resources of a large area of the so-called Third World to the Western bloc was consequently never disputed, although the United States was always cautious not to be too closely identified with British imperialism. It is conspicuous, for instance, that the main American grievances against European imperialism, British in particular, invariably centred on protective and preferential economic practices which discriminated against the United States. Soon, the United States itself would penetrate the vacuums created by the decolonisation process, substituting economic or military control,[27] as would the European powers, for direct political overlordship in these areas. Indeed, so far as neo-imperialism was concerned, the American Grand Design differed from the larger British purpose mainly by its reference to an American controlled North Atlantic industrial-military axis as the centre of gravity for the non-Communist world.[28] Containment thus meant contradiction and imperial rivalry—a reliance on Britain's imperial world role which conflicted with its ultimate end of an Atlantic community so organised that, among other things, the United States would have equal access to the resources and markets of territories marked off by European imperialism; and a reliance on Britain which, in terms of the elevation of the Anglo-American alliance, served to bolster Britain's illusions of her postwar status, thereby increasing her resistance to European unity.

By the middle of 1950, the United States realised its misplaced optimism in British leadership of the European movement, that the British Labour Government would go no further than mere 'cooperation' and entertained no intention whatsoever of surrendering an iota of its sovereignty to European unity. American disappointment was first engendered by the British attitude towards the OEEC as an instrument for European integration. The Americans supported French and Benelux interest in establishing an independent organisation invested with some effective powers, but largely through British opposition, shared by the Scandinavian countries, the OEEC eventually emerged as a weak inter-governmental organisation. The British attitude to the Council of Europe was even more frustrating. The Statute of the Council of Europe, signed on 5 May 1949, was a diluted version of federalism removed almost beyond recognition from the original proposal of French Foreign Minister Georges Bidault, which called for an all-European consultative assembly whose members would be elected by the national parliaments, and who would exercise an independent vote. The Statute was another compromise between French and Benelux inclinations towards independent supranational organisations and British insistence on loose inter-governmental forms. Britain finally accepted a Consultative Assembly only after ensuring its subordination to a Committee of Ministers, as the sole body to which the Assembly could report, and that only in recommendatory form, besides which it controlled the matters for discussion by the Assembly.[29] As if to guarantee the impotence of the Council of Europe, the unanimity rule obtained in the Committee of Ministers, which met as an inter-governmental forum, and whose recommendations were themselves only of recommendatory force to the individual member governments.[30] Anglo-American differences over institutional forms, with Britain's preference for weak organisations, were reflected in sharp disagreements even at the level of individual appointments. Largely through British persistence, and without American backing, Robert Marjolin, considered in Washington as a lukewarm Europeanist, was appointed Secretary-General of the OEEC in 1948. This caused much annoyance in Washington, which supported Ambassador Harriman's preference for Jean Monnet, although Monnet himself was known to be a somewhat reluctant candidate. Similarly, while the British preferred Dr Stikker, the Americans endorsed the more radical Henri Spaak for President of the Consultative Assembly of the Council of Europe. Spaak, also President of the OEEC from its inception, was, moreover, being urged by Ambassador Harriman, during the autumn of 1948, to resign as Belgian Premier and 'head up (the) OEEC in an effort to give greater vitality to movement for increased unity',[31] presumably at the expense of Robert Marjolin as Secretary-General. Subsequently, in January 1950, following Spaak's increasing public criticism of British 'foot-dragging', the British Government decided it 'should tell [the] US Spaak is not acceptable . . . as "OEEC Superman" '.[32]

In both the cases of the OEEC and the Council of Europe, British reservations in accepting the challenge of leadership towards European unity were a source of keen disappointment to the American Administration. An important factor in shaping American attitudes towards Britain was, of course, the socialism of the British Labour Government.[33] The conflict between British policies and those conceived to be in the interests of European integration[34] was a constant source of Anglo-American friction during the ERP. Americans were both suspicious about socialism and contemptuous of what they perceived to be a futile attempt by the Labour Government to re-create some primordial utopia. Final disillusionment with Labour came with Britain's rejection of the Schuman Plan.[35] Yet, despite the subsequent shift in focus from Britain to the Continent for leadership of the European movement, the Administration still retained some hope that Britain, under the Conservatives, would find her place within Europe. Churchill, after all, had been vociferously advocating European unity,[36] and the Conservatives in Opposition had taken the Labour Government to task for its negative attitude on European unity. The realisation came swiftly, however, that the Conservative Government was certainly no less intransigently opposed than its predecessor to European unity. The main American annoyance was that Britain would have her cake and eat it too—that she would like to maintain Imperium and have one foot in Europe; that she would neither go fully into Europe, nor let Europe go, giving the continentals the necessary encouragement to proceed on their own towards unity. This disappointment over Britain's unchanging stand on European unity was to lead to a re-examination of American policy approaches towards Western Europe, and eventually, by 1956, to a profound shift in the United States' attitude concerning Britain's relations with Western Europe.

Britain under the ERP

Britain's economic relations with Western Europe between 1948 and 1956 were set within the framework of the OEEC and, until its termination in 1952, the European Recovery Programme. It was inevitable, however, that Britain's economic policies towards Western Europe would be significantly influenced by her major economic, political and military international role, especially in relation to the Commonwealth and to the sterling area. On this account any attempt to view Britain as being entirely, or principally, within a Western European nutshell would necessarily create serious problems and frictions over British relations with Western Europe. Yet, this was the prevailing United States attitude as expressed by the ECA in its efforts to encourage integration among the OEEC countries. To further complicate the problem of American attitudes, there were besides the ECA's European integrationist outlook, two other perspectives towards Britain. There was the residual multilateralist philosophy of the Treasury, and secondly, there was a tendency towards an Anglo-American special relationship coming from the State Department. Differing perspectives and functions, together with inadequate coordination among these bodies in the operation of United States foreign economic policy, displayed a certain ambivalence in official attitudes and policies concerning Britain's role.

The collapse of expectations for a rapid transition to recovery and international economic equilibrium, and the growing ideological division and new political tensions in the world, succeeded in temporarily paralysing any major progress toward the American multilateral ideal for the postwar world.[1] From the spring of 1947 the main American concern was tackling the problem of European recovery, which had generally been seriously underestimated in its planning for the postwar international economic system. But the horizons of the ECA, as a specially appointed fully independent body responsible for the administration of the ERP, were from the outset severely limited by its blinkers of Western European economic recovery and integration. The ECA, firmly backed by Congress, was primarily concerned with marshalling the OEEC countries into economic integration. Britain was to be no exception. On the other hand, the Treasury Department was quite sceptical of the regional integrationist approach of the ECA as being inconsistent with its own economic philosophy. The real difference between the perspectives of the Treasury and the ECA related to the advisability of advancing multilateralism on the regional scale in Western Europe without adequate provision for its subsequent extension. The Treasury still retained its fundamental universalist multilateralist perspective on economic matters, and it looked forward to its application as soon as possible throughout the Western world. Regionalism savoured of economic discrimination and divisiveness; permanent recovery was necessary to restore international equilibrium as a prerequisite to multilateralism; but while the liberalising economic policies being pushed through by the ECA were, with the exception of the European Payments Union, warmly welcomed by the Treasury, it consistently feared the possibility that a general expansion of multilateralism might be contradicted by the establishment of a protectionist integrated Western European economy. The internationalist mould of the Treasury in outlook and activity naturally held its implications for Britain, chiefly in terms of seeing Britain as a primary factor within the international economic system. The role of Britain as an indispensable pillar in the future multilateral order, rather than as an important peg in an integrated Western Europe, marked the difference in perspectives between Treasury planning for the postwar world and the ECA approach to Western Europe. Admittedly, American Treasury officials had never been able to see eye to eye with Britain on economic policies, and they provided an unbroken genealogy of varying degrees of Anglophobia with Secretary J. W. Snyder himself uncompromisingly so. A long-standing source of serious friction were the American criticisms of the protectionist and discriminatory trade and financial policies of the Commonwealth and the sterling area. Indeed, the State Department's determination do away with imperial preference had been a major obstacle to Anglo-American agreement on the abortive ITO;[2] while in the drafting of the Atlantic Charter of 1941, and more specifically in the terms of the

Mutual Aid (Lend Lease) Agreement of 23 February 1942, as well as in the Anglo-American Financial Agreement of 6 December 1945, the Americans had exacted commitments from Britain to order her postwar policies according to the ideal of universal multilateralism.[3] Of more recent vintage was the deep-seated abhorrence of the socialist programme of the British Labour Government for its rigid central controls, seemingly excessive state intervention in the private sector, nationalisation, and large expenditure on the social services. Nevertheless, despite the basic antipathy towards the Labour Government, and to Britain's Commonwealth and sterling area policies, the Treasury fully recognised the existence of the dollar and sterling as 'key' currencies in the international economic system. This conception was inescapable in the lengthy friction-ridden Anglo-American collaboration and joint planning for Bretton Woods and Havana, and it was the governing consideration behind the Anglo-American Financial Agreement of December 1945, which was seen as an instrument for expediting Britain's postwar recovery along multilateralist principles, in order to commence the proper operation of the new elaborate financial institutions—the International Monetary Fund and the International Bank for Reconstruction and Development.[4] Although the loan ultimately produced the reverse effect, and although the British convertibility crisis of July–August 1947 dramatically brought home to the United States the chronic economic weakness of Britain, there was no fundamental change in the Treasury's philosophy. Thus, during the ERP the Treasury remained anxious to progress towards its conceived multilateral economic order, and although from the standpoint of its primary concern with the monetary system it consistently demanded major changes in British policies, it was prone to focus with rather marked conservatism on Britain's traditional role associated with the world-wide circulation and international respectability of sterling.

The State Department was traditionally concerned mainly with the commercial aspects of foreign economic policy. From Cordell Hull it had tenaciously embraced the multilateral faith, and played the main part in the Anglo-American commercial collaboration for the postwar order. Naturally, its perspectives on economic matters had constant and emphatic reference to political considerations. This was particularly the case after the collapse of American plans for the postwar world, when it recognised the imperative of rebuilding Western Europe economically principally as a bulwark against Communism. Secretaries Marshall and Acheson were content to follow the ECA's path towards European integration, not only because the State Department shared the ECA's and Congress' interest in a dynamic European market for American goods and investments, but because their political interest in ultimate European unity accepted the argument that economic integration was a necessary prerequisite. But in so far as political-military considerations were at the bottom of the State Department's outlook, it recognised, particularly under Acheson, the indispensability of the Anglo-American relationship as the main strength of the West. The importance attached to the Anglo-American alliance and the long-term interest in European unity placed the State Department in an especially ambivalent position towards Britain under the Truman Administration. The fundamental conflict lay in the simultaneous tendency to support the ECA's efforts to push Britain into European integration, while acknowledging a special position for Britain in the context of Western defence. Moreover, the overriding preoccupation with defence saw the State Department acutely concerned about Britain's economic position in a manner that made it at times, such as the devaluation crisis of 1949, incline to a special economic relationship with Britain. Besides the recognition of the vital importance of British strength, Anglophile sentiments within the State Department between 1947 and 1953 created a predisposition for general collaboration, akin to the war-time cooperation and the joint approach in Bizonia, even though the prevailing approach in the economic sphere was to include Britain in Western European integration. Seen by the ECA then, Britain was but part of Western Europe, on equal footing with the continental countries and falling within the integrationist framework: in the view of the Treasury, Britain was a distinct entity in the wider international economic system, heretical in policies and a reluctant but necessary pillar of multilateralism: for the State Department, Britain was basically within the European integrationist scheme, but sometimes qualified for special emergency attention within the Anglo-American relationship. On this general sketch of official attitudes, however, it was the ECA which, from 1948 to 1952, exercised the greatest influence in United States policy concerning Britain's economic relations with Western Europe.

In his address before the OEEC in July 1948, ECA Adminis-

trator Paul Hoffman appraised the European situation and charted
the course towards integration:

...The Organisation for European Economic Cooperation has been
in existence now for approximately three months, and our American
Economic Cooperation Administration for a little over three and a
half months. ...

It is time to take stock in broad and basic terms of our objectives
and of our present position in relation to those objectives. Most of
that stocktaking must be done by you – I can perhaps make a
contribution by reporting as accurately as I can upon the present
attitude of the American people toward the European Recovery
Programme.

A substantial majority of the American people, President Truman,
and Mr. Thomas E. Dewey, candidate of the Republican Party, all
our great labour organizations, business organizations and farm
organizations enthusiastically support the European Recovery Programme. But this should be noted: the support of the American people
stems from their belief in your pledge as set forth in the Report of
the Committee of European Economic Cooperation and later reaffirmed by you in the Convention for European Economic Cooperation. In the Convention for European Economic Cooperation,
participating countries pledged themselves 'to combine their economic strength to join together to make the fullest collective use of
their individual capacities and potentialities' and to 'undertake the
elaboration and execution of a joint recovery program' in order to
'achieve as soon as possible and maintain a satisfactory level of
economic activity without extraordinary outside assistance'.

To the American people and I am sure also to yours, this pledge
has a very real, a very simple meaning. I should like to focus
attention on three elements of the pledge which was made: the
promise of joint action and collective use of your capacities and
potentialities ; the responsibility of each nation to develop an inclu-
sive program in the fields of sound government finance, production and trade ; and the terminal date. ...

While there has been a growing conviction that it is in the
deepest interests of the United States that Europe should again become a living, workable and independent economic and political
organization, there has at the same time been a growing conviction
that this goal cannot be set in the frame of an old picture or
traced on an old design. It cannot be brought about by old ways
of doing business or through old concepts of how a nation's interests
are best served. New patterns of intra-European trade and exchange
must be found and new directions in the use of Europe's resources.
These are made necessary and not alone [by] the drastic conse-

quences of two wars, but also by the tides of change that run longer and deeper.

Each participating nation, looking at the operations of its own national life, must face up to readjustments to satisfy the requirements of a new world. These readjustments cannot be made in the course of national action along the old separatist lines. They can only be accomplished if each nation seeks its new goal in terms of the economic capacity and the economic strength of Europe as a whole....

... It is the responsibility of each government to develop its own program, and [it] is the responsibility of each government to work out the mutual adjustments which will be the basis for a master plan.

What seems to me to be called for and quickly is such a master plan of action based upon the full recovery of the European economy by June 30, 1952, when American aid terminates. This master program would, of course, be a composite of programs developed by the sixteen participating nations, Western Germany and Trieste. I want to make clear as crystal the fact that what I have in mind is a program of action, not a rigid and ponderous five-year plan which tries to compress the life processes of a nation into a set of formulae and a sheaf of statistical tables....[5]

British leadership was expected in the formulation and implementation of the American-sponsored European 'master plan'. But after the prompt initiative of Bevin in rallying a European response to Secretary Marshall's Harvard Address, United States officials, particularly in the ECA, and the United States Special Representative to Europe, Ambassador Harriman, were to be sorely disappointed by the subsequent British attitude within the OEEC. The American dismay at Britain's insistence on the OEEC being a weak inter-governmental organisation when some of the continental countries were ready to invest it with a major degree of independent power was only the prelude to serious conflicts over Britain's economic policies. These conflicts mainly occurred in the form of the ECA pushing integrationist policies on the OEEC and Britain staunchly resisting them. In a situation where the Americans tended to assume that the continental countries would naturally follow British leadership, it was especially frustrating for them to find Britain 'dragging her feet' while France, Italy, and the Benelux countries appeared willing to progress along integrationist lines. The consequence was a growing division within the OEEC between the timid approaches of Britain and the Scandinavian countries on the one hand, and the more cooperative multilateral inclinations of the middle continental countries on the other. The Americans invariably supported the latter while exerting substantial pressures behind the scenes on Britain to make more radical departures and set the pace for European economic integration.

During the course of the ERP, American officials tended to place much of the blame for the cautious OEEC approach to integration on Britain. This was almost as much the case on the State Department side as it was on the ECA, although the former was generally more sympathetic towards Britain's difficult position of reconciling herself to a diminishing role. In the earliest stages of the formulation of the Marshall Plan, Assistant Secretary of State for Economic Affairs, William Clayton, had impressed upon Secretary Marshall the central position of Britain in European integration. In a memorandum addressed to the Secretary after Clayton's return from Europe in May, he wrote:

> This three-year grant to Europe should be based on a European plan which the principal European nations, headed by the UK, France and Italy, should work out. Such a plan should be based on a European economic federation on the order of the Belgium-Netherlands-Luxemburg Customs Union. Europe cannot recover from this war and again become independent if her economy continues to be divided into many small watertight compartments as it is today.[6]

But the posture which Britain was later to adopt in the councils of the OEEC was promptly indicated in Anglo-American discussions in London, following almost immediately upon the Harvard Address. These discussions lasted three or four days and were between Clayton, Ambassador Douglas, Bevin, Dalton, and Cripps. The main concern of the British officials was with 'impressing on [Clayton] that we are something more than just a bit of Europe'.[7] This was obviously quite difficult, and the British Government's position was set forth in an aide-memoire covering the talks which was subsequently circulated in Washington:

> Public opinion in the US attaches importance to an assurance by the countries of Europe that their goods and products of all kinds will be available to each other so that the needs of Europe will, so far as is economically practicable, be met from European resources and this should be reflected in the pattern of reconstruction and development. US opinion is thinking of a continental rather than a country approach to the present trade and production problem of Europe.

First reaction of UK officials to this is: any proposal for assurances even in principle that European countries would constitute themselves into a Customs Union would present great difficulties and almost certainly involve delay which, in present circumstances, would be disastrous.

On the other hand, as there is a shortage of essential resources for capital re-equipment, there is scope for considerable cooperation between countries in order to avoid unnecessary duplication of effort in capital expenditures.

It must be recognised, however, that schemes for integrated production must carry some security for the producer that he will have an assured market and to the user that he will obtain supplies. The working out of this conception presents considerable difficulty. But it probably presents the natural line of evolution towards the conception of continent of European viable economic unity [*sic*].

Moreover, the position of Great Britain, which is not merely a European country but an international trader presents special difficulties.[8]

This conflict between an American interest in integrating the British economy with continental Western Europe, and the British claim to a special position vis-à-vis the Continent and a 'special relationship' with the United States was fundamental. The special position of Britain had been recognised in the Anglo-American planning for the postwar economic order, but it was repudiated in the planning for the ERP. The terms of the Anglo-American Financial Agreement of December 1945 had seriously tried to cut the grass from under the Commonwealth and the sterling area in the interests of multilateralism.[9] The Agreement attacked the sterling area dollar pool; demanded the free convertibility of sterling within a year; required Britain to ensure that countries holding sterling balances either scale them down or refund them; prohibited quantitative discrimination against American imports; forbade British credit from Commonwealth countries on terms more favourable than those of the Agreement (i.e. two per cent per annum); and ushered Britain into the Bretton Woods institutions. The paradox of the Agreement was that, while it was based on a recognition of Britain's special economic position, it would in effect have placed Britain on her own in a multilateral Western economic régime by provisions which would have undermined the fundamental basis of Britain's special position, namely the discriminatory Commonwealth and sterling area relationship. At the same time, although the loan acknowledged Britain's economic

'key' role and assumed the necessity of Anglo-American collaboration, it was not from the American side based on any
recognition of a 'special' Anglo-American relationship, which, in
any case, would have been at odds with the multilateralist philosophy.[10] In such circumstances, when in the spring of 1947
American attention was attracted to the real crisis of the economies
of Western Europe, and multilateralism was put by the board in
favour of a massive European recovery programme, it was not
too difficult for the Americans to see the opportunity of reorientating Britain's historic economic relationships away from
Commonwealth and sterling area and towards Western European
economic integration. This was justified in the rationale of regionalism, and in the assumed necessity of the full participation of the
British economy in any economic resurrection of the Continent.
The British, on the other hand, continued to stress their special
position and to plead for 'special' consideration. In the midst of
the British convertibility crisis in the summer of 1947, Dalton
records that:

> E.B. [i.e. Bevin] has been sending some very good telegrams to
> Washington including some explosions to Ambassador Douglas. The
> latter has been dining a lot at the House of Commons with various
> groups of M.P.'s and telling them all that there is no chance of
> Congress doing anything at all before March and no chance then
> of their doing anything special for the U.K. as distinct from Western
> Europe.[11]

In Britain's search for special consideration under the Marshall
Plan and for amelioration of the loan terms, the attitude of Congress was of course decisive, and decidedly anti-British. Dulles
privately confirmed, though with guarded pessimism, Ambassador
Douglas' judgement of the Congressional mood:

> As regards the loan terms, the Administration will, I think, make
> all the concessions possible without Congressional action, but some
> things probably cannot be done without a vote of Congress and
> that cannot be until next year [i.e. 1948], and it is not safe to predict
> now what the temper of that Congress will be.[12]

The convertibility crisis itself, which saw the transferable con-
version of an estimated $300 million from sterling during the
period 1 July to 20 August 1947,[13] when convertibility was sus-

pended by Anglo-American agreement, fully exposed the weakness of the British economy and only served to obscure to Americans any relative difference between the economic weakness of Britain and that of the continental countries. Accordingly Britain's membership of the OEEC and participation in the ERP was interpreted by the ECA as well as the Administration as the beginning of the end of the Anglo-American 'special relationship', and the beginning of Britain finding her place in Europe.

The ground of conflict between the United States and Britain in the operation of the ERP had thus been laid, for Britain was by no means ready to find her place in Europe. The economic policies of the Labour Government were firmly set in their traditional framework. British cooperation within the OEEC was made all the more difficult by the Labour Government's overriding preoccupations with achieving national recovery and the welfare state. Whereas the other European countries were beginning to see their economic future in increased intra-European cooperation, the British Government looked to doctrinaire Socialism on the national level, and its established Commonwealth and sterling area relationships on the international. The determined aim of United States policy, however, was the economic integration of Western Europe including Britain, and Acheson, in 1950, recognising the importance of rapid progress towards European integration, 'found it extremely difficult in view of the attitude of the British Labour Government and the difficulty of their reconciling integration with the socialization and planning needed for their domestic policies'.[14]

It had been hoped that by making the OEEC responsible for the distribution of American aid, the necessary cooperation among the participants would provide a basis for strengthening the organisation and for an overall joint programme of action towards integration. The general official American attitude saw the OEEC, in the words of Senator Lodge, as 'the practical symbol' of European economic unity, and the dual purpose of recovery and integration which was attached to the organisation is very aptly expressed by the Senator in the following passage:

I think there are a great many Americans whose enthusiasm for this whole concept [i.e. European unity] will be governed by the extent to which the OEEC increases in influence and authority. I think there are many people in this country who regard that as

D

the plus, as distinguished from the minus aspect of this thing which is vitally important. Of course, the minus is the dropping of communism. The plus is the extent to which Europe integrates itself, and the OEEC is the symbol of that unification....[15]

Unfortunately, there was to be sour disappointment about the achievements of the OEEC apropos the 'plus' aspect. The attempt of the OEEC countries to agree on a 'master plan' was early abandoned after their long-term programmes insisted on by the ECA proved quite irreconcilable.[16] Thereafter the approach was step by step, each weighed by strenuous negotiations, in tackling the fundamental obstacles to maximising intra-European trade. The problems centred on two basic issues, payments and trade. The postwar monetary and commercial policies of the Western European countries were marked by their rigid exchange controls and harsh import barriers. No less than two hundred trade and payments agreements had been negotiated among the Western European countries by the end of 1947.[17] Bilateralism, protectionism, non-convertibility of currency would severely limit the value of any aid to Western Europe, and the main assault of the ECA was consequently on behalf of rapid payments and trade liberalisation.

Limited steps were taken by the OEEC countries towards an intra-European payments agreement during the summer of 1948, with seventy-eight sets of bilateral negotiations finally culminating in the Agreement for Intra-European Payments and Compensations of 16 October 1948.[18] The essentially bilateral character of that Agreement was naturally quite unsatisfactory to the ECA, which in the following year succeeded in having the Agreement revised toward some degree of genuine multilateralism by transferability of drawing rights.[19] This was followed by the ECA proposal in December 1949 for a European Payments Union, which after lengthy negotiations was finally agreed to by the OEEC countries in July 1950.[20] The other major question of trade liberalisation was attacked from two angles. In the first place, the OEEC countries eventually agreed among themselves to a progressive removal of quantitative restrictions, deciding in November 1949 to set an initial goal of fifty per cent reduction on their existing quotas. By this time, however, Hoffman and his ECA associates were pressing for a rapid advance towards integration, and sought a scheduled eighty per cent liberalisation over a year with the complete disappearance of quotas by the middle of 1951.[21]

Under ECA pressure, the OEEC countries decided in January 1950 on an eighty per cent stage to be reached after the creation of the EPU, and in October 1950 the OEEC Council adopted a seventy-five per cent liberalisation goal applicable to total imports, to be attained by the beginning of February 1951. The previous levels of agreed quota reduction had been related to specific categories of imports—food, raw materials, manufactured goods—but agreement on the seventy-five per cent stage would not have been reached on this basis mainly on account of opposition to further quota reductions in the agricultural sector. In April 1951, however, the OEEC Council accepted a 'common list' of commodities on which quota reductions were to be removed by all the OEEC countries, excepting Germany and those which had still not reached the sixty per cent stage.[22] The progress of the OEEC in tackling quantitative restrictions certainly expanded the flow of intra-European trade in a wide range of commodities. But any overall assessment of the OEEC policy would have to take into account the extent to which removal of quotas was offset by tariff restrictions; the implication of applied statistical criteria of volume of trade in relation to the actual range of commodities liberalised in each country; and, particularly in the case of Britain and France, the proportion of state trading in the total flow of national imports.[23] As for the OEEC's subsequent efforts on the issue of tariff reductions, no appreciable success was made here at all.[24] The OEEC had largely preoccupied itself with quotas until in the middle of 1950 the low tariff countries, particularly Belgium, began forcing the question of tariff reduction as a necessary complement to further removal of quotas. Lengthy negotiations toward some form of agreement within the framework of the General Agreement on Tariffs and Trade (GATT), signed in October 1947, were without result. Various suggestions for an OEEC preferential tariff area were equally fruitless,[25] while the issue on the whole tended to be overshadowed by the Schuman Plan and the changing emphasis from recovery to rearmament occasioned by the precarious international situation following the outbreak of the Korean War. Altogether, very little was accomplished by the OEEC in the context of the 'plus' aspect of its function. In his letter of resignation to President Truman in September 1950, ECA Administrator Paul Hoffman carefully summed up his attitude concerning OEEC's progress after two and a half years:

... while the nations participating in the Marshall Plan have with ECA aid gone far in rebuilding their economic strength much remains to be done. And now that the nations are facing the urgent need of expanding sharply their armed forces and increasing their production of war material the further strengthening and the integration of their economies have become essential.[26]

The main conflicts that arose over Britain's policies under the ERP concerned the vexing issues of trade liberalisation and the European Payments Union. During the first year of the ERP, the OEEC had made no real progress towards the freeing of intra-European trade and payments, which had been completely subordinated to individual problems of national recovery. Advance at this level had been generally satisfactory, and in the case of Britain substantial. Exports of the continental countries in 1948 had risen to just below the 1938 level, while Britain's had considerably surpassed it. In the year ending June 1949, Britain's balance of payments on current account had recouped remarkably and had achieved a rough equilibrium, with exports for the period climbing to forty-five per cent above the prewar level and imports falling twenty per cent below.[27] The general progress in national recovery was viewed by Hoffman as 'a good start, but only a start towards recovery', and he was anxious to emphasise that:

What remains to be done will be harder and far more significant for the permanent strength of free Europe.... From the ECA point of view, the real proving period lies ahead. We can now say with assurance that Europe is through the first phase of its economic recovery. In the months ahead Europe must tackle the more difficult problem of making major readjustments which break away from its traditional—and now inadequate—ways of paying its way in the world.[28]

The ECA was immediately concerned with the liberalisation of trade in the interests of increased competition and efficiency in production, lower prices for essential commodities, and as the first step towards integration. With the end of the first year of ERP allocations approaching, the ECA had to present Congress with evidence of tangible progress towards European integration. It was to Britain among the OEEC countries that Hoffman and his associates looked for the initiative in trade liberalisation. The Labour Government, however, remained preoccupied with its national programme and resisted arguments for trade liberalisation, on the ground that its national recovery was still incomplete. The British held that liberalisation should await full economic recovery and the achievement of an assured favourable balance of payments. Firm internal domestic controls and protection from outside competition would be required for the proper reconstruction of the British economy for some time yet. Moreover, the British were as keen as ever to point out that their economic relationships were centred elsewhere than in Europe—in the Commonwealth and the sterling area—and could not be properly regarded without reference to that fact, despite Britain's membership of the OEEC. Unfortunately, it was precisely this situation that the ECA was determined to change in telling Europe that it must 'break away from its traditional—and now inadequate—ways of paying its way in the world'.[29] Under severe pressure and insistence from Hoffman, who 'had it out with Cripps', and who told the OEEC members that if they did not take steps towards liberalisation by 1 May he could not report to Congress on a satisfactory degree of European self-help and mutual cooperation, the British Government finally took the initiative.

On 3 June 1949, the OEEC Council favourably received the proposal of the British Chancellor of the Exchequer, Sir Stafford Cripps, for the progressive removal of quotas on intra-European trade. In reluctantly taking this forward step, Cripps also moved sideways by underlining his opposition to any liberalisation which might incur losses to Britain in gold or dollars,[30] while indicating that British action depended on reciprocal response from the other OEEC members. The initial OEEC reaction to the British proposal was somewhat suspicious, as it came during the deadlocked negotiations on the revised payments agreements of 1949–50 when Britain was adamantly opposing transferability of drawing rights.[31] But the proposal was nevertheless accepted and formed the basis of the OEEC's intra-European trade liberalisation programme, agreed to at the end of June 1949 and gradually extended.[32] Although by October 1949 Britain had freed quotas from approximately sixty-six per cent of her 1948 private intra-European trade,[33] the restrictions which had been swept away were carefully selected from quotas covering a range of commodities which could be imported without too detrimental an effect on Britain's balance of payments and economic planning. Moreover, in accordance with Cripps' warning, the list submitted

to the OEEC for the lifting of British quota restrictions did not
extend reductions to Belgium, West Germany, or Switzerland, for
fear of gold and dollar drain.[34] At the same time, the increasing
role of state trading within the British economy was hardly over-
looked by the ECA as a severe qualification of the sixty-six per
cent figure, subsequently increased to over eighty per cent, in
terms of Britain's total volume of European imports. Nevertheless, the British proposal was received by the ECA as a step,
'mini-step' though it was, in the right direction and accepted as
probably the best it could hope to exact initially.

The question of intra-European payments was a far more dis-
ruptive issue. The ECA proposal in December 1949 for a European
Payments Union constituted a radical departure from the previous
intra-European payment plans.[35] Although its basic function remained the same, that of providing an arrangement for covering
intra-European trade deficits without payments constantly running
on gold or dollars, the ECA plan called for the creation of a
flexible multilateral clearing-house system of payments, with automatic balancing of net credits and deficits among the several
participating countries by reference to each country's 'quota' in the
Payments Union.[36] Settlement of EPU accounts would be between
the individual Governments and the EPU, assessed in terms of each
country's net balance in relation to all the others and its 'quota'
in the EPU. Thus, if a country was a net debtor, depending on
the extent of its deficit, it would receive partial credit from the
EPU and be required to pay the remainder of its deficit in gold or
dollars to the EPU:[37] conversely, a creditor country would receive part payment in gold or dollars from the EPU and credit
on account with the EPU, the relative proportions varying with the
amount of net credit. The EPU was the brain wave of the ECA,
which 'pushed the matter aggressively' on the OEEC countries,[38]
but apparently without prior approval of the United States
National Advisory Council on International Monetary and Financial Problems.[39] The upshot was undisguised conflict over the
implications of the ECA proposal. There was no quarrel over the
mechanics of the proposed institution, but Treasury officials, in
particular, were opposed to the EPU, on the grounds that it conflicted with the wider international multilateral ideal represented
by the IMF.[40] Their greatest fear was that in so far as the EPU
represented a step towards regional convertibility, it might further
postpone the attainment of world-wide convertibility, with an

attendant discrimination against the United States by the creation in Europe of 'a regional soft-currency area which is protected from United States competition by trade restrictions and which develops an artificial economic structure within its walls'.[41] The EPU proposal in fact brought to a head the ambivalent strands in United States foreign economic policy represented mainly by the Treasury, on the one hand, and the ECA and the Department of State on the other. And the confrontation mushroomed into a general rethinking of the pros and cons of European economic integration:

> None of the agencies [i.e. on the National Advisory Council] seems to believe that a European clearing organisation will not overcome barriers to commerce or stimulate intra-European trade. Neither do they argue that the Clearing Union advocated by the ECA is badly designed from a technical point of view and that as a consequence it will not work. Their lack of enthusiasm for the European Payments Union appears to arise not from any misgivings as to its ability to attain its objectives, but rather from a questioning as to whether the United States should strive for these objectives. They are apprehensive that the building of an integrated Europe will necessitate the maintenance of barriers which will keep United States exports out of the European market and which may delay the attainment of world-wide convertibility.[42]

The ECA got its way, however, with Congressional approval for the establishment of a European Payments Union. But the controversy within official American circles was demonstrative of the divergence still existing in the Truman Administration's postwar policy. A divergence which was not simply related to economic considerations, but from the State Department's standpoint rested fundamentally on political, military, and strategic considerations pertaining to the strength which would accrue to the West out of an economically integrated Western Europe with vast overseas resources. Provided an integrated Western Europe remained pro-American, discrimination against American goods would be a small price to pay for the creation of a situation of strength centred on a dumb-bell Atlantic axis, around which the greater proportion of the world's resources in men and raw materials orbited.

The highly-charged conflict between the United States and Britain over the latter's resistance to participation in the EPU revolved around rival politico-economic conceptions of the postwar organisation of the West. The essence of every British argument against the EPU was the detrimental effect which it might have on sterling and on the sterling area.[43] Sterling and the Commonwealth constituted the twin pillars of Britain's traditional world role. While the Labour Government was prepared to increase its international influence by cooperation with Western Europe, it had not the least intention of sacrificing the majesty of imperium for statehood in a united Europe, or risking the sterling nexus for the nominal convenience of an intra-European accounting mechanism when most of its essential trade was within the Commonwealth and sterling area. The greatest apprehensions of the British Government were that the existing substantial sterling balances, together with any subsequent acquisitions of sterling from overseas non-sterling area countries, might be deposited in the EPU with the effect of increasing Britain's gold and dollar liabilities. The British wanted some arrangement for reconciling the sterling area with the EPU before participation in the latter. There was the fear that the continuing role of sterling as a major international currency might eventually be threatened by the EPU, both in terms of curtailing the use of sterling and in the possibility of defections from the sterling area, should the units of the EPU become a recognised international currency.[44] Certainly, this was one of the main suspicions in the official American attitude concerning Britain's opposition to the EPU:

> The situation of the United Kingdom does, however, raise some large issues. The sterling area is itself a payments union. England apparently believes that her future as a world power depends on maintaining her position as centre of the sterling area. Consequently, all of the discussions so far have contemplated the inclusion of the entire sterling area in the European Payments Union, although it would be represented only by the United Kingdom.... This creates a problem, insofar as one of the objectives of the Payments Union is to promote European integration.... Furthermore, there is some feeling that the British fear the European Payments Union as a rival to the sterling area. The political ties that hold the sterling area together are in most cases tenuous and in some cases have disappeared.... If a European Payments Union should become a major factor in world commerce, it is possible that certain countries might desert the sterling area and join the European group. It may be that eventualities of this nature influence the British attitude toward the ECA proposal.[45]

When, after much persuasion, Britain eventually decided to join the EPU, Sir Stafford Cripps was anxious to assure the House that:

The Government have been naturally concerned, throughout the discussions leading up to the present agreement, to ensure that an improved payments scheme for Europe should not be secured at the expense of weakening the position of sterling as an international currency. We are satisfied that the position of sterling is adequately safeguarded in the proposals that have now been adopted and that we need not fear any detriment to our wider interests.[46]

Throughout the EPU episode, Britain was under constant American pressure. In the first place, Hoffman had been rather unduly optimistic about the success of the proposal, prophesying in January 1950 that agreement would be reached within ninety days.[47] Such a schedule, of course, was not entirely coincidental with the Congressional consideration of further ECA allocations due in March. The British position was considered the main stumbling block, and Hoffman saw it, described before the Senate Foreign Relations Committee, as 'torpedoing our efforts toward achieving an integrated economy in Western Europe'.[48] It was made quite clear to Britain that if she did not join the EPU the faucet of American aid to her would be turned off. In requesting a new appropriation of $600 million from Congress, Hoffman stated the intention that:

A part of this sum will be used to support a proposed European Payments Union and the balance will be made available directly to the qualifying countries.... If in the first instance some nations say they cannot join for some particular reason, it simply means they do not get their proportionate share of the $600,000,000.[49]

Deputy Administrator Richard Bissell subsequently underlined the point before Congress.[50] At a different level Ambassador Harriman had earlier had a direct confrontation with Cripps over Britain's attitude on payments. These were 'very tough talks', in which the United States Special Representative found that he 'had never argued harder with any man than Cripps apart from Molotov.' Perhaps the barrage of public American criticism of Britain's rejection of the offer to participate in the Schuman Plan negotiations, and the unbridled American hostility to the publication of the Labour Party pamphlet 'European Unity'[51] might have also aided Britain in seeing her way into the EPU. The Labour

Government had postponed decision on the EPU until after the British general elections in February 1950, in which they were returned to power. Initially, the British Government had insisted on the retention of their bilateral trade and payments arrangements, by which means they hoped to offset the worst disadvantages which might befall their economic system by participation in an automatic payments union. In pressing for this and the limited administrative manoeuverability which it implied vis-à-vis the non-negotiable operational system of the EPU, the British Government was prepared to forego its right to borrow from the EPU while fulfilling its obligation to lend to it.[52] Britain was also very wary about the credit policies which the EPU might adopt and desired that the Union give credit only after a country had surpassed the credit margins of its bilateral arrangements.[53] This proposal would have subordinated the flexible multilateralism of EPU financing to bilateral agreements in such a way as to safeguard Britain's bilateral agreements with various continental countries governing the use of sterling. A compromise was reached in the negotiations by the provision of an optional clause which provided for the alternative of bilateral credits, to a country's credits either to or from the EPU, on condition that such credits did not increase, decrease or in any way alter its overall creditor or debtor position in the EPU.[54] In effect, this meant only that the members of the EPU could resort to bilateral agreements on sterling with Britain. But the real advantage which Britain had sought, namely the employment of bilateral agreements on sterling credit to give her advantages in trade terms, was offset by the condition attached to the exercise of the optional clause, in that whatever bilateral agreements were reached, they could not alter one jot Britain's net position in the EPU. However, there is perhaps some point in the claim that while it was more of a concession by than to Britain, it was nevertheless such a concession 'as is necessary to have an "international currency" '.[55] A further compromise was that while Britain eventually agreed that the holdings of sterling balances of EPU members on 30 June 1950 could be used for the settlement of net deficits in the Union, the ECA undertook to recover to Britain any losses in gold or dollars that such action might incur on Britain.[56] This agreement on the part of Britain was not too difficult to make in view of the fact that the countries likely to have net deficits with the EPU were precisely the ones that held the smallest sterling balances.

When the EPU Agreement was signed on 19 September 1950, Britain had joined as a full participating member. The EPU was the most significant achievement of the ERP in terms of progress towards Western European economic integration. Unrelenting American pressure for British participation in the EPU provided the fullest confirmation of the United States conception of the reorientation of Britain's economic role towards its inclusion in Western European integration. The ground for this had been laid by the extension of the Marshall Plan to Britain on the same footing with the continental countries, by British membership in the OEEC, and by the persistent American sniping at the discriminatory practices of the Commonwealth and the sterling area. But a very fundamental question remains to be asked. Considering that in the interests of permanent European recovery, maximum productivity, higher standards of living, and a large European market, the United States aimed at including Britain in Western European economic integration, precisely what conception did the United States have of the future relationships of the Commonwealth countries and of the British and other European colonies to this economic unity of Western Europe? Keen insight into American attitudes on this issue is gained from general Congressional discussion on the ERP. In proposing before the Senate, in March 1948, an insertion to the Economic Cooperation Act of 1948 to make it explicit that the United States wished 'to encourage the political unification of Europe', Senator Fulbright submitted 'as a very persuasive argument' in support of the insertion the following statement of Prime Minister Smuts, of the Union of South Africa, 'one of the great statesmen of our time, a practical man of politics ... who understands world affairs, as few men in the world understand them': quoted in part, the statement reads:

When I look at the world situation, I think first of the necessity for saving and rebuilding Europe. Europe is the heart of our world problem today. Europe is the traditional centre of the civilised world. It holds the great concentration of brilliant peoples who have made the modern world, the centres of commerce, the wells of culture. Beside it the problems of the rest of us are not of the same order of urgency.

But Europe is sick, very sick. . . .

That is why I think the Marshall Plan is of the first importance. It brings the resources of the United States to the rescue of Europe where necessary. . . .

But the Marshall Plan is not enough. It is only the beginning.
Material aid alone will not save Europe. Europe needs a spiritual
awakening – a hope to hold on to. That hope is closer cooperation
and union – a western union such as Mr. Bevin [Ernest Bevin, British
Foreign Secretary] has suggested and to which the British Government is now committed. A governing concept is needed, a vision
of the new Europe which will appeal to the imagination and a new
clarion call to its suffering peoples.

In that union Africa can also play her part. Africa is divided into
territories nearly all of which belong to or are allied to the nations
of western Europe. Africa and America are affiliated to Europe,
to the western company of nations.

Africa, like America, can supply the resources needed to rebuild
Europe, and the Union of South Africa in particular is rich in the
things which Europe requires. Our special contribution here to the
pattern for peace will be to protect and develop our agricultural,
mineral, and industrial wealth and, in collaboration with the great
territories to the north of us, to produce the things which will help
Europe to live again. . . .

We may have the western union, made up of western Europe and
Britain – the English Channel has ceased to have significance. Africa
and North America have their links with that union. Then we may
have the Slav bloc, consisting of European and Asian Russia, and
all her satellite countries. Thirdly, there may yet arise what you may
call the far eastern bloc, the exact shape of which it is still too early
to discern clearly.

But it would be a mistake to think that this division of the world
means war.[57]

If the implications of American interest in European integration
on the role of the Commonwealth and the European colonies are
not clear enough, the able Senator from Arkansas, whose views
consistently had the support of Senators Lodge and Thomas in
representing the majority Congressional attitude on European
unity, provided further light on the subject by the inclusion for
the record of an article entitled 'The Great Design'. Here the
important point being made is that

The 16 Marshall-Plan nations comprise a population approximately
twice as great as that of the United States. They are people of great
energy, possessing a vast assortment of trades and technical skills,
and their nations are collectively rich in agricultural and mineral
resources.

What they lack at home, they have access to in their colonies and
commonwealths across the sea. In its book, *World Minerals and*

World Peace, the Brookings Institution shows that the European nations—Britain, France, and Holland in particular—are far from underprivileged as compared with the United States when foreign possessions are counted.

If these countries could join together to pool their resources and their markets, they would have the opportunity to achieve cheap mass production and a high standard of living, such as prevails in the United States.[58]

Further clarification of the anticipated position of the European empires under the ERP is given by Representative Powell, with explicit reference to the American legislation. Rep. Powell opposed the ERP 'because it will not help Europe as it needs to be helped' and because 'it will further enslave millions of colonial peoples throughout the world, and notably in Africa'.[59] In addressing the House of Representatives, he endeavoured to point out that 'it is impossible to give a proper evaluation of the European Recovery Programme without taking into account the colonial implications and consequences of that proposed programme';[60] as it was, however, he went on to show that that was precisely what the Administration had done. He argued that:

Britain, France, Belgium, Netherlands, and Portugal are imperialist powers. They are the rulers of well over two-thirds of the 300,000,000 colonial subjects of Asia, Africa, and the West Indies.

Throughout modern history, the peoples and resources of these lands have been exploited to enrich the ruling class of the colonial overlords. . . .

A valid economic aid program for Europe cannot be based, as the administration sponsored ERP is, upon continued and intensified colonial exploitation.

America should help the European people to help themselves. . . .

The abject poverty and resultant social stagnation characteristic of all colonial countries are the inevitable consequence of their being held by stronger powers to supply cheap raw materials. The expropriation of their resources and the wealth produced by colonial labour is what keeps colonies poor.

Instead of helping to eliminate this vicious system, the ERP has the effect of perpetuating and strengthening it.

The Outline of European Recovery Programme submitted by the Department of State for the use of the Senate Foreign Relations Committee, December 19, 1947, states—page 19—that paragraph (5) of subsection 10 (b) of the proposed economic cooperation bill 'is designed to assist the United States wherever feasible to obtain materials for stock-piling purposes. Such materials will be purchased from a participating country or its colonies or dependencies, either through private contracts or through the procedures and with the funds authorized in the Stock-Piling Act. It is intended that arrangements will be worked out with the participating countries for the acquisition by the United States in the above manner of materials which will be specified in the bilateral agreements.'

The meaning of this is made clearer on page 48 of the same document, where we read:

The United States has few or no domestic sources of certain raw materials, such as tin, industrial diamonds, natural rubber, and quinine, and has inadequate resources in other raw materials, such as manganese, chromium, copper, lead, and zinc.... United States reserves of exhaustible natural resources are declining. It is proper that in partial return for the very considerable assistance provided them by the United States, the participating countries should give reasonable help in replenishing stocks of materials expected to be in long-term short supply in the United States.

Not all of the participating countries themselves possess sources of such materials. Some among them do, however, have resources of this nature, either within their own territory or that of their colonies, territories, or dependencies. In some instances present production and availability is at maximum levels without satisfying commercial demands. In other instances it appears that, under an aggressive plan of exploration, development, and expansion of productive facilities, or by other actions, additional supplies could be produced or made available....

That is the picture of what the ERP means for the colonies of Britain and the other European imperial powers. Not a very pretty picture—all take and no give....

Let us face the truth honestly and admit that the United States Government is today the mainstay of world imperialism....

In helping Britain, France, Belgium, and the Netherlands to hold on to their empires, Wall Street and Washington aim to keep the far-flung colonial empires, as well as their European rulers as allies against Communist aggression, and incidentally safe for American profits.[61]

It is perhaps important to underline that there is no essential difference between this statement and the previous ones concerning the relationship of the European colonies to European integration under the ERP. The differing moral perspectives behind the statements must not be confused with the analyses of the main issue, which are identical. Whichever statement is read, the fundamental point which emerges is that under the ERP it was expected that:

the European colonies in Africa, Asia and elsewhere must serve the function that they have always served, but in a bigger and better way than hitherto, for they must now provide the raw material needs not only of their European rulers, but of America as well.[62]

The problem which beset the United States and Britain in regard to the latter's resistance to European integration was basically that the British Government hoped to make the best use of the Commonwealth and Empire for maintaining its own international position. This was to be done in conjunction with the continental countries of Western Europe closely organised under British leadership—it was, of course, Bevin's declared view that 'we are entitled to organise kindred souls in the west just as they [i.e. the Russians] have organised kindred souls in the east'.[63] The point is, however, that Bevin's contemplated Western Union—'the formation of a Western European entente having as one of its primary aims the promotion of inter-imperialist collaboration in the intensified exploitation of Africa and other European colonial domains in order to rescue Europe from economic bankruptcy'[64] —would not assure the United States of the anticipated free and easy access to Commonwealth and colonial resources and markets resulting from the integration of the British economy in Western Europe. This, together with the creation of a large European market for American goods, was seen as the *quid pro quo* for Marshall Aid. American historical opposition to British imperialism was after all mainly an opposition to its economic discrimination against the United States. And not only Lend-Lease and the Loan Agreements, but Marshall Aid itself, provided America with the opportunity of rectifying the situation in its own favour. Hence the perplexity of Mr David Eccles in informing the House of Commons that 'for reasons which we all know but do not understand, the Americans approve of the Commonwealth when talking about defence but disapprove of it when talking about trade and finance'.[65] Mr Eccles, speaking on American aid and the European Payments Bill of January 1949, both made and missed the point concerning the underlying conflict between Britain and America over the Commonwealth and the ERP. He said:

It is easy to see where the British and American policy went wrong. The Commonwealth ought to have been brought into this picture much earlier and much more intimately, as I have said in this House on many occasions. The flaw in the policy is that the Marshall Plan does not reflect the fact that the whole project of European recovery breaks down without the raw materials of the sterling area. What should we have done about this? ... For reasons which we all know but do not understand, the Americans approve of the Commonwealth when talking about defence but disapprove of it when talking about trade and finance.

When His Majesty's Government saw the consequences of this American attitude they ought not to have eaten humble pie and kept quiet. They should have gone over to the offensive and said to the United States that, because of their policy about off-shore purchases, it was only as an organised Commonwealth that we could play our full part in the Marshall Plan. They ought to have said to the Commonwealth that if they considered the sterling area was something worth preserving—and we all know that they do—they should join with us at once in working out under the wing of ECA a junior Marshall Plan.[66]

The case was not, however, that American policy 'went wrong', rather that the speaker did not fully appreciate the intentions of American policy. But it is difficult to disagree with his view that in terms of preserving the traditional British imperial role, the British Government might have insisted on the inclusion of the British Commonwealth and sterling area in the ERP, or have sought to devise a 'mini-Marshall Plan' among themselves. The latter alternative was probably not quite practical, however, while the Labour Government might be excused for not having done the former in view of the fact that in the circumstances in which the ERP evolved, the element of strict European economic integration was initially overshadowed by the priority of recovery. But there is no escaping the divergence between the perspectives of the United States and Britain over the latter's postwar role. This divergence very much revolved around the role of the Commonwealth, the colonies, and the sterling area. From the British point of view these were the sacred pillars of her strength: from the American, they should be opened up together with other European overseas territories for American interests and should be the raw material basin and strategic outposts of a 'dumb-bell' Atlantic community, including Britain in a united Western Europe. Thus in his statement before the House Committee on Foreign Affairs during the Hearings, on 8 February 1949, on the second year's programme of the Foreign Assistance Act, Ambassador Harriman found himself

... increasingly impressed by the long-range importance of the development of the dependent oversea territories of the participating countries and of the vigorous resumption of American private investment abroad. 'I mention these together because it seems likely that the active development of the resources in these territories could be substantially effected by American private investment, and that one of the most constructive opportunities for American private investment abroad would be in the development of such resources.' Such a plan would not only make possible the desired increase in America's stockpiles of scarce raw materials, but 'would also have a wider significance.' There was an increasing need to assure future sources of supply for the growing requirements of American industry. 'As American industry continues to expand and its productivity continues to increase, the volume of raw materials needed from foreign sources will grow larger. The dependent oversea territories now produce many of these materials, and their potential production is far greater. In the development of raw materials in these territories, and in the encouragement of private American investment to assist in this development, new and stable cycles of trade and investment would emerge. This seems to me one of the most promising ways to assist in reaching a balance of payments.'

Mr. Harriman claimed that 'a comprehensive and co-operative effort by the participating countries and the United States along these lines would also help carry forward the progressive development of these territories in the interest of their inhabitants in accordance with the principles of the United Nations Charter.... These are common problems which call for a common program among the European countries involved.'[6]

The inconsistency in official American attitudes, reflected in the effort to fit Britain into Western European economic integration while recognising the overriding importance of Britain's independent traditional world role as a factor of immediate significance in the military-strategic security of the West, is most discernible by analytic comparison of United States economic and defence policies towards Britain in the context of the European movement. But it is apparent even within the economic sphere. After its brief respite during the first year of the ERP, the British economy was once again, in the late summer of 1949, undergoing serious balance of payments difficulties. Chancellor of the Exchequer, Sir Stafford Cripps, estimated that all Britain's reserves

E

would be consumed within about twelve months from June 1949, engaging the possibility of 'a complete collapse of sterling'.[68] Conversations with American officials on the recession, on devaluation, and on convertibility had been taking place throughout June. Little headway was made. The British officials felt that their opposite numbers in the United States were quite unable to grasp the simple problem of Britain's reserves—dollar drainage through adverse balance of trade with the United States—and that their own American recession was also partly to blame for much of Britain's new troubles.[69] On the other hand, the American Administration, especially in the persons of Secretary Snyder and his financial advisers, was convinced that the pound sterling ought to be devalued, and gentle persuasion was tried to set Britain on such a course.[70] While it was not United States policy to risk having to accept part of the blame for any ill effects of a British devaluation, and therefore the Administration made it well understood that the decision lay only with Britain,[71] the Americans well knew that, provided they offered no relief to the British crisis, then Britain would soon be obliged to take the necessary step. In any case, the patently unsympathetic attitude of Treasury officials and of Congress, which had all along been hypercritical of the Labour Government's socialist experiment, effectively ruled out any prospects of immediate assistance. This was fully appreciated by the State Department, which inclined to be the most cooperative, and Acheson was aware that any untimely proposals to come to Britain's rescue while Congress was facing the Atlantic Pact, Military Defense Assistance, and the extension of appropriations for the ERP, would certainly occasion 'an explosion on the Hill'.[72] Towards the end of August, the British Government tentatively reached its decision to devalue the pound. But as a preliminary step, it called the Washington Tripartite Conference of 7 September 1949, to confer with the Americans and Canadians on such action.[73]

According to Kennan, although the Tripartite talks were officially conducted in the name of the United States Treasury, this was 'to satisfy the suspicious anti-Anglicism of upstanding figures on Capitol Hill'.[74] In fact, it was the Department of State which exerted the primary influence from the American side. The Department of State could not allow the American response to the British crisis to be straight-jacketed by the Treasury's fiscal focus and myopic Anglophobia, which did not take into account the

Department of State's primary consideration of the vital connection between Britain's economic buoyancy and Western security. Acheson was concerned about British strength.[75] George Kennan, as head of an inter-departmental recommendatory committee for the talks, approached them with the recognition that:

> At the present moment, with a great question mark hanging over the solidarity of Russian rule in the satellite area and with an extremely tense and unpleasant situation in the Far East, it would be catastrophic if anything happened to disrupt the spirit of confidence and solidarity and the reality of economic stability and progress in the Western world. This, however, was exactly what would happen if something drastic were not done about the British situation. . . .[76]

But this diplomatic logic behind the State Department's Anglo-American outlook during the talks is nowhere more dramatically expressed than in the following remarks of Senator Hubert Humphrey for the *Congressional Record* on the opening of the Tripartite Conference:

> Make no mistake about it. Britain is our one and only powerful ally. An insolvent and impoverished Britain will be a liability. A solvent, productive Britain can act as our outer fortress. A breakdown in Anglo-American relations at this time would be a victory for Joe Stalin second only to the conquering of all of Western Europe. . . . I know that those who do the negotiating for the United States Government understand the importance of further American assistance in this crisis. Her economic difficulties, if left unchecked, will be but a forerunner of a much more severe economic collapse in the North Atlantic area. . . . Britain is the keystone to our North Atlantic defense system. It is military stupidity and economic madness to permit the major power in our system of alliance to become imperilled because of a dollar crisis.[77]

At the opening of the Tripartite Conference, Britain informed the United States and Canada of her intention to devalue the pound sterling. Public announcement of British devaluation was not, however, made until 18 September, almost a week after the talks had ended. Naturally, many of the continental European countries were considerably irritated by the way in which devaluation was unilaterally announced—the feeling that Britain had been called into a separate conference in Washington while her continental partners in the OEEC simply had to await the decision which was sprung upon them some time after the conference.

France in particular was sour about her exclusion from the talks.[78] Despite the fact that the Washington talks had been at the invitation of the British, they were hardly 'forced upon' the Americans as Kennan might make out.[79] Rather the case was quite simply that in its own anxiety over Britain's economic situation, the State Department gave little consideration to possible continental reactions to the Anglo-Saxon talks from which the decision to devalue emerged. Secretary Acheson's subsequent plea that the Washington talks should not be interpreted as implying any change in United States policy concerning European economic cooperation provided little balm for hurt French pride, and merely served to further underline the ambivalent attitude of the Administration towards Britain. For in the Washington Tripartite Conference the three powers agreed to joint action to restore a satisfactory balance of payments between the dollar and sterling areas, and in the communiqué following the talks this was represented as being of fundamental importance to the 'free-world', as the dollar and the pound sterling remained the two principal currencies.[80] Both the special consideration given to Britain's economic plight in the Washington talks, and the various personal Anglo-American discussions which preceded it, as well as the conclusions reached in the talks, indicate the State Department's basic recognition of the inseparability of Britain's economic position from her role within the Anglo-American alliance as the immediate mainstay of the West. Hence the inherent ambivalence of the State Department's position which, while supporting the integrationist policies of the ECA towards Britain, would also adopt an Anglo-American approach which acknowledged the 'key' currency concept and the traditional British economic framework as being fundamental to Western security. Accordingly, from the State Department's standpoint, economic arguments in favour of British participation in European economic integration existed side by side with the political logic and military necessity of supporting Brtain's world role based on precisely the 'traditional—and now inadequate—ways of paying its way in the world' that Hoffman was determined to eradicate.

The extent to which some officials in Washington were prepared to give Britain separate and preferred treatment seems to have had virtually no limit at the time of the British dollar crisis in August-September 1949. An outstanding example is the contemplation in State Department quarters of an eventual economic merger between Britain and the United States. This line of thinking received the greatest prominence in an article in the *Wall Street Journal,* which both reveals the details of the proposal and provides an insight to the undercurrent of Anglo-Americanism in the State Department perspective:

> An economic union of the United States and Britain. That startling idea is being seriously discussed privately by a growing group of key State Department officials as 'the only way out' of Britain's 'permanent' dollar shortage. These officials think Britain could but won't solve her own problems. For political-military reasons, they figure, the United States must solve them for her permanently.... Whether it matures or not, this sensational proposal is significant, for it shows how little faith the administration now has that England can be rescued by any mild or temporary aid.... This all adds up to the proposition that the two countries should merge their economies almost as completely as those of the 48 United States. Yet the two nations would keep their political independence. How this could work out is a question the State Department men have not quite cleared up....
>
> Those who are discussing economic union say the idea is politically impossible right now. But as one of them argues 'it may not be later'....
>
> These men (i.e. proponents of economic union) answer that Britain's recovery is the key to European and world recovery....
>
> These same men declare the United States must depend on Britain as a military kingpin in the Atlantic Pact. They say if Britain weakens, the pact loses much of its value....
>
> It is argued that expanding the area of free trade would give producers bigger and more lucrative markets.... Officials hope the free trade could gradually be extended throughout the Commonwealth— to Canada, South Africa, India and other regions totalling a fourth of the world's area.[81]

As the article correctly observed, this thinking was not then 'official State Department policy',[82] but was merely under consideration. In fact, the chief architect of the proposal was George Kennan, who had the support of the Policy Planning Staff. The idea of some kind of US–UK–Canadian economic merger had been Kennan's from as early as the formulation of the Marshall Plan.[83] During the British economic crisis of August-September 1949, he pushed such an arrangement with renewed vigour, chiefly from his own esoteric conception of an Atlantic community constructed around an Anglo-Saxon bloc, on the one hand, a united Western

European continental grouping to the other. Thus, in his analysis
of British economic problems to Secretary Snyder and Under-
Secretary of State James Webb, during August 1949, in preliminary discussions on the American position at the forthcoming
Tripartite Conference, Kennan strongly advocated the limitation of
Britain's role as banker of the sterling area and British participation in the closest economic relationship with the United States
and Canada:

> I pointed out that their [i.e. the British] dollar drain arose from
> two factors: (a) their position as banker for the sterling area and
> (b) the adverse UK balance of trade with the dollar area. As to the
> first, I suggested that perhaps they ought to cease trying to be the
> bankers for at least a portion of the sterling area.... As for the
> British adverse balance, that was a question of adjustment of the
> British economy to the economies of North America, and I thought
> that we ought at least to agree to join them in appointing a commis-
> sion of inquiry to determine what institutional changes, if any, might
> be made in the relations between the three countries (US, UK,
> Canada), which would ease this adjustment and prevent each single
> component of it from being made a particular issue and bone of
> contention in the relations between the respective countries.[84]

Kennan, however, did not see the possibility of very much being
done to help the British in the short run,[85] and contemplated a
special US–UK–Canadian economic relationship as an eventual
goal of American policy. While he entertained no doubt that the
'harsh, boorish, shortsighted' 'anti-Anglicism' of Congress[86] ruled
out the immediate practicability of his objective, it was nevertheless his hope that the Administration would be willing to give it
serious consideration in the future. Consequently, his main disillusionment occasioned by the 'elaborate antics' behind the inter-
departmental American approach to the Washington talks came,

> ... first, as a revelation of the difficulty that would obviously be
> involved in trying to find understanding among Washington political
> circles for anything resembling *a close and collaborative association
> with the British, much less anything approaching a union with them
> and the Canadians....*[87]

Yet, closer examination of Kennan's overall approach reveals what
is perhaps illustrative of the kind of inconsistencies generally found
in official American circles at the time on the question of Britain's
relations with Western Europe. For it is difficult to understand how

he managed to reconcile his idea of a US–UK–Canadian union with his 'dumb-bell' conception of Atlantic community—'the combination, that is, of a unit at the European end based on the Brussels pact, and another unit at the North American end—Canadian–United States, this time—the two units being separate in identity and membership. . . . .'[88]

Neither Kennan nor his planning staff had any major influence on United States policy while Acheson was Secretary of State.[89] Acheson himself certainly never contemplated the idea of a US–UK–Canadian economic merger and passed it by as another masterful display of the intellectual acrobatics of the Policy Planning Staff. Yet, despite his explicit denial that such a proposal was part of American policy, Acheson acknowledged that officials had been considering 'how Britain's economic problems would be affected by a "closer relationship between the two countries" '.[90] This in itself amounted to an admission of the ambivalence in the American attitude towards Britain, characterised in the Anglo-American approach of the Washington Tripartite Conference against the background of constant American pressure for Britain's economic integration with Western Europe.

The preoccupation of the ECA with European economic integration was eventually overshadowed by the effective switch in Truman policy from European recovery to rearmament, following upon the outbreak of the Korean War. This shift, and the ending of any distinction between aid for economic purposes and aid for defence which accompanied it, occurred while general European recovery was still incomplete, and was embodied in the philosophy behind the Mutual Security Act of 1951 which directly related future aid to the defence efforts of the recipient countries.[91] Until that time, however, the control and influence of the ECA over American foreign economic policy ensured that the regionalist economic approach held sway. As the years passed, however, the division among the OEEC countries over the pace and manner of progressing towards increased unity visibly widened. The middle European countries—France, Italy, the Benelux, and Western Germany—were growing apart from Britain and the Scandinavian countries. Britain's attitude on the Schuman Plan, in May 1950,[92] and later on the proposal for a European Common Market fully indicated that her position on integrating her economy in Western Europe had not changed. At the same time, the American acquiescent response to the British rejection of the Schuman proposal further demonstrated the ambivalence towards Britain's relations with the Continent.[93] As one commentator ruefully put it:

The United States sometimes lumped Britain with the Continent in urging European unity, Britain being so lumped in the Marshall Plan. At other times the United States has given Britain separate and preferential treatment ever since its loan to Britain 2 years before the Marshall Plan.[94]

As far as British policy was concerned, an interesting verdict is provided in the following comment of Senator McCarran, Chairman of the Foreign Aid 'Watch Dog' Committee:

My point is that the record shows that every time the British Government has been offered an opportunity to join other Marshall-Plan countries in concrete action towards the unification of Europe, the British Government has not only failed to assume leadership, but has obstructed and delayed the actions of others.

This was true of those efforts made from time to time to give authority to the OEEC—the organization of the Marshall-Plan countries. This was true of the attempt of the continental countries to create the European Payments Union.... And now we see the familiar pattern being followed in the current effort to unify the European steel and coal industries.

All these British positions, I believe, can be explained simply. The fact is that in spite of the many policies the United States has in common with the United Kingdom, despite the great good will which the two nations have for each other, the British objectives with respect to European integration are fundamentally opposed to those of the United States.

Our foreign policy since the end of the war has assumed that British and Americans were partners in a common enterprise, striving for a common objective. While I do not doubt that the British agree with us on such obvious ends as peace and the general welfare, it seems clear they do not agree on the immediate steps for rebuilding the economy of Europe....

... While we have many more interests in common than we have differences, the British do have a Socialist Government and the British are trying to hold together the Empire.[95]

NATO and the supremacy of the Anglo-American alliance in defence

When Ernest Bevin set about the creation of the Brussels Treaty Organisation in the winter of 1947–8, this was only a first step. His real goal was a multilateral Atlantic security system as a framework for the revival of the Anglo-American alliance, and as a means of permanently involving the United States in the defence of Western Europe in order to underpin effectively his Western Union design. Bevin's conception of the evolution of an Atlantic security system differed from the French-Benelux approach to the BTO as a nucleus for an essentially Western European regional defence system to which it was hoped the United States would eventually give its support by way of a direct treaty commitment. Considering American interest in European unity and support for the BTO as a major step in that direction, the logical American course, when it came to making a security commitment to Western Europe, should have been in line with the French-Benelux approach. Almost from the outset, however, United States policy on this major issue was pushed in a different direction both by Bevin's diplomacy and by the shortsighted tactics of the Truman Administration in its responses to the pressures of internal American politics. The eventual outcome was the North Atlantic Treaty Organisation. But primarily on account of its multilateral character NATO provided a natural framework for the predominance, until the middle fifties, of the Anglo-American alliance as the central pillar of Western defence, at the expense of active British leadership in the development of an integrated Western European defence arrangement which was in fact the real aim of American policy.

The formation of the BTO was carried out with full American backing and on the understanding that the European effort would receive credible American support as soon as it effectively came into being. On 13 January 1948 Bevin informed the United States of his interest in creating 'some form of union in Western Europe, backed by the Americans and the Dominions',[1] and the response was very encouraging. The only significant reservation was that the Administration with its focus firmly set on European integration pressed for a regional defence arrangement in Western Europe along the lines of the Rio Treaty[2] rather than support Bevin's proposed network of bilateral alliances among Britain, France, and the Benelux countries. When on 17 March 1948 the Brussels Treaty was signed, President Truman welcomed it before a joint session of Congress, saying that 'it is a notable step in the direction of unity in Europe for protection and preservation of its civilization. I am confident that the United States will, by appropriate means, extend to the free nations the support which the situation requires'.[3]

With the agreement on the Brussels Treaty, a decisive step had been taken, but somewhat more tangible evidence of European self-help was required before the United States could consider the precise nature of the support it would give to the European undertaking. According to Under-Secretary Lovett, the State Department 'insisted that at least some practical measures should be taken by these countries on their own as an earnest of good intentions before consideration would be given by the United States of any military pledges....'[4] Towards the end of April, with establishment of the machinery of the BTO under way, the State Department considered that as a result of its earlier insistence, 'practical steps were being taken for consolidating the military preparations of the five Brussels Agreement Countries and that a point had now been reached where in the Department's opinion the United States would have to formulate its position'.[5]

At the core of the American problem in trying to decide on some kind of pledge of support to Western Europe was the question of the form such a pledge should take. Should it be a unilateral declaration of commitment, like the Truman Doctrine for instance, or, alternatively, a formal treaty commitment? If the latter, which should be the approach—a direct treaty commitment with the BTO, or a multilateral Atlantic regional collective security treaty? Secretary Marshall, Lovett, and John Foster Dulles in particular, who was a leading Republican spokesman in the initial 'bipartisan' discussions of NATO, were quite aware of the problems surrounding a formal commitment and of the serious shortcomings of the regional formula under Article 51 of the United

Nations Charter as the vehicle for commitment.[6] The main quarrel with it came from Dulles. He raised the possibility of a party to the treaty subsequently becoming Communist, and argued that any formal, permanent, or long-term commitment would arrest developments towards European unity. There was sympathy for Dulles' views from Marshall and Lovett, both of whom also sensed a certain 'artificiality' in applying the regional concept under Article 51, notwithstanding quite basic historical and civilisational trans-Atlantic ties. However, from their point of view, when all was considered, it seemed to be the only acceptable formula.

The genuine security anxieties of the Western European countries, particularly of Britain and France, and the fall of Prague in March 1948, were instrumental in the Administration's conclusion that only full and formal commitment to Western European defence would deter further piece-meal communist expansion, and ensure the atmosphere of security in the region necessary for its recovery. At the same time the United States was under constant pressure from Britain, supported by Canadian inclinations, for participation in a regional compact under Article 51 of the United Nations Charter. The susceptibilities of the United States to arguments framed in the context of the Charter were fully appreciated and thoroughly exploited by Britain. Bevin well knew that that was possibly the only route for United States association in a peacetime alliance, and he recognised how much the public conscience of the Charter had influenced the American insistence that the BTO should be of multilateral regional collective defence character if it were to receive American support. Accordingly, Article 51 was Bevin's main gambit. Posed in terms of the weaknesses of the UN's security provisions, and of the consequent need for a Western anti-Communist coalition, instead of endeavouring to repair the peace-keeping machinery of the UN, Bevin's arguments rang a particularly convincing note in Washington, especially after the Czechoslovakia coup. In the view of one commentator, 'Article 51 provided a convenient "umbrella" for what, ironically enough, amounted to side-stepping the UN's defence system'.[7] In his approach, Bevin had the consistent support of the Canadian Secretary of State for External Affairs, Mr Louis St Laurent, whose influence in Washington, as Bevin knew, was not inconsiderable, Canada being viewed by Secretary Marshall as the 'connecting link between the United States and north-western Europe'.[8]

On 28 April 1948, Mr St Laurent had proposed before the Canadian House of Commons what essentially amounted to NATO,[9] and had from as early as September 1947 suggested in an address to the United Nations General Assembly that the impotence of the Security Council might be circumvented 'by an association of democratic and peace-loving states' within the framework of the United Nations' Charter.[10] From the standpoint of Bevin's conception of Britain's ultimate role, and his need for inducing the United States into an Atlantic defence system as the basis for developing Western Union, he had good reason to rejoice in Mr St Laurent's prognostications and understandably agreed that 'nothing could so successfully reinforce the Charter' as a world-wide system of regional defence arrangements.[11] More directly, Bevin spared no effort in drawing the attention of the United States to the various 'risks' involved in any other commitment than a formal one based on an Atlantic regional concept. Truman recalls the following:

> The principal risk involved, Bevin said, was that the Russians might be so provoked by the formation of a defence organization that they would resort to rash measures and plunge the world into war. In this, our experts agreed with the British. On the other hand, if a collective security system could be built up effectively, it was more than likely that the Russians might restudy the situation and become more cooperative.
>
> The British Foreign Secretary also pointed out that an Atlantic security system was probably the only way in which the French could be brought to agree to a rebuilding of Germany. Such a system would give all the free nations of Europe the sense of confidence they needed to build peace and prosperity in the world.
>
> Bevin thought that to be effective the security arrangements must carry *real assurance* for the nations of free Europe.... He then expressed the opinion that it would be very difficult for the British, or other free nations, to stand up to new acts of aggression unless there was a *definitely worked-out arrangement, which included the United States,* for collective resistance against aggression.[12]

In the circumstances of American politics in 1948, once the Administration had decided on some kind of formal treaty arrangement with Western Europe, the path led almost willy-nilly towards Article 51. This was the line of least resistance if not indeed the only line of action. The American constitution prohibited peacetime alliances, and the situation was further considerably complicated both because 1948 was the Presidential election year, and on account of the already existing legislative difficulties presented by a hostile Republican 80th Congress, with strong isolationist predispositions.[13] Considerations of international image, and of allaying accusations of aggressive intentions,[14] as well as the need to placate strong sentiments in the Senate still upholding the aspirations of the UN,[15] suggested a certain wisdom in operating within the framework of Article 51. For another influential section of Congressional opinion, collective security would at least have the appeal of seeming to provide something in return for American efforts—not another of those 'one-way arrangements in which [the United States] did something for foreign countries without receiving anything in return'.[16] Bipartisan discussions during April had clearly revealed that these considerations weighed heavily with the one man who could win the support of the Republican Senate for a formal commitment to Western Europe, Senator A. H. Vandenberg, leading Republican spokesman on foreign affairs and Chairman of the Foreign Relations Committee. Vandenberg's interest was first of all in having a formal peacetime commitment which would pin down the Administration to far-reaching Congressional action, in which he well knew that he would have the leading role. His personal view was that a regional pact legitimated within the Charter of the United Nations would of all alternatives have the least difficulties in Congress. When, in May 1948, a final decision was reached in favour of working for a regional Atlantic Pact, an important tactical consideration was that the Senate's current interest in the question of general reform of the United Nations could be a useful vehicle for a resolution nominally on that subject but primarily intended as a constitutional ground-breaking for the North Atlantic Pact. This was the approach developed within the Administration which clearly preferred to ride on the back of the tiger than to risk getting inside, by attempting to push any alternative to the regional multilateral formula whatever its logical deficiences might be. In the ensuing bipartisan 'ball game' the Administration's tactics were fully assisted by Vandenberg's personal vanity, and as the price for his cooperation in carrying the Senate his was to be the historic occasion and glory.

The Vandenberg Resolution was passed by an overwhelming

majority on 11 June 1948, and paved the way for the Atlantic Pact through its historic provision for 'association of the United States, by constitutional process, with such regional and other collective arrangements as are based on continuous and effective self-help and mutual aid, and as affect its national security.'[17] Preliminary talks on the North Atlantic Treaty followed from July to September, against the turbulent background of the Berlin blockade, and the North Atlantic Treaty was eventually signed on 4 April 1949, to be ratified by its twelve participants on 24 August 1949.

In formally committing itself within the North Atlantic Alliance the United States had accepted a multilateral Atlantic collective security framework which was somewhat inconsistent with its original interest in the BTO as a significant step towards closer regional cooperation in Western Europe and the nucleus of a Western European defence arrangement. Logically, a straight American commitment to the BTO would have been more consistent with the aim of American policy in promoting Western European integration, and it would have gone farther to facilitate the development of a two-pillar Atlantic community. Nevertheless, viewed simply in terms of a vehicle for formal United States commitment to Western European security, American acceptance of the multilateral North Atlantic Alliance might not in itself have had some of the results which it did. The real problems of the association began to emerge when the Atlantic Pact sought to transform itself into a collective defence organisation.

In seeking to tie the United States in an Atlantic Pact, British foreign policy aimed not only at extracting a formal American commitment to Western European security, but at actively involving the United States in the defence of Western Europe within a multilateral Atlantic defence organisation, in which it was envisaged that the Anglo-American alliance would be predominant. Neither the British nor the Continentals considered an American commitment as being in itself an adequate guarantee of Western European security, and the French in particular were always prone to stress that the real issue was not American commitment to *ex post facto* liberation of Western Europe, but American commitment as an act of deterrence which necessarily involved active American participation in Western Europe's defence arrangements. On the other side of the Atlantic, the United States had regarded its commitment within the North Atlantic Treaty principally from the standpoint of the need to allay Western European anxieties by an explicit American assurance of the principle of collective security. Such an assurance was considered necessary for proper progress in the European recovery effort, parallel to which Western Europe was expected to rebuild its own defences within the BTO framework and with the support of large-scale American military aid under the Mutual Defense Assistance Program of October 1949. Thus the United States initially looked at the North Atlantic Pact more in the sense of a collective security arrangement, as in the Rio Treaty, than in terms of the establishment of a full fledged defence organisation except as a very long-term possibility.

The North Atlantic Treaty did not itself explicitly provide for the creation of a defence organisation, but only for the establishment of a Council (under Article 9) empowered to 'set up subsidiary bodies as may be necessary' and to 'establish immediately a defence committee'. When the NATO Council held its first session on 17 September 1949, it established the Defence Committee, and a Military Committee with a Standing Group comprising the United States, Britain, and France, and in addition to these it set up Regional Planning Groups for five regions of the Atlantic. But this was still a far way from an Atlantic defence organisation, for at this stage of its incubation NATO was geared to no more than trying to formulate general plans for harmonisation of the separate actions of its members in the event of a crisis. For fifteen months after its establishment the North Atlantic Alliance remained in this form, as Acheson describes it 'a body—or more accurately twelve bodies—without a head'.[18]

The inadequacies of NATO were fully recognised in Western Europe. The successful testing of an atomic device by Russia in September 1949, and the mounting Russian military presence in East Germany maintained the level of anxiety in Western Europe about security. The critical point was reached towards the middle of 1950 with the outbreak of the Korean war in June, and the accompanying fear—sustained by influential 'Fortress America' and 'Asia First' elements in the ensuing Great Debate within America—of a shift in emphasis of United States policy which would subordinate the question of European defence to developments in the Far East. This apprehension and the genuine dissatisfaction with the ineffectiveness of NATO gave rise to increasing insistence, particularly from the French supported by the British, on American troop movements to the Continent, and an integrated defence under NATO with a unified command and positioned forces at the ready. In August 1950 Prime Minister Attlee visited President Truman and tried to impress upon him Britain's and the Continent's inability to meet the economic burden of additional defence needs in Western Europe, even on the existing scale of American military aid, without much direct American involvement. But while the United States recognised the urgent need for a far greater rearmament effort on both sides of the Atlantic, the Truman Administration, which was beginning to embark on its H-Bomb programme, could not seriously expect that Congress would be prepared to carry the cost of economic recovery and rearmament in Western Europe, on top of the increasing expenditures which the American defence effort would itself be demanding. The Truman Administration, which was anxious to place Western European defence squarely on its own footing within the Atlantic Alliance, approached the problem from two directions, one of which called for greater cost-effectiveness through the proposal of balanced collective forces which had been accepted after considerable debate at the Fourth NATO Council meeting in London, in May 1950. The other approach was through German rearmament.

The issue of German rearmament was one of the most perplexing problems which faced the United States and Western Europe during the fifties.[19] Although by 1950 the United States had convinced itself that the rearmament of Western Germany within the Atlantic Alliance was essential to Western European defence, it took fully four years before a practical and acceptable formula could be found for rearming Germany. The main impetus for German rearmament came from the Department of Defense which lost no time in convincing the State Department that this was the central problem to be overcome in establishing effective European defence. In the months after the outbreak of the Korean war, the American military establishment, which was gaining increasing influence over United States policy, was particularly insistent on the rearmament of Germany as the condition to be laid down for any direct commitment by the United States on ground and air forces to Western Europe and on integrated defence within NATO —involving a unified command, a Supreme Commander, and common strategy.[20] This was the position adopted by the United States in the so-called 'one package' proposal put forward in the Tripartite Talks among Secretary Acheson[21] and Foreign Ministers Bevin and Schuman, and submitted to the NATO Council, meeting concurrently in New York, in September 1950. The French were pathologically opposed to German rearmament and Schuman's reaction to the 'one package' proposal was, after attempting in vain to separate its contents, absolute rejection. Bevin's position, however, was somewhat different. For although he had his own misgivings about German rearmament, and had to cope with intransigent opposition within the Labour Party and British public opinion to such a course, not only were his own Chiefs of Staff coming to accept German participation as an indispensable element in the establishment of a viable European defence, but from the standpoint of the larger objectives of British foreign policy under his leadership, German rearmament hardly seemed too heavy a price for the permanent integration of the United States in the defence of Western Europe. Thinking mainly in terms of the direct inclusion of German units within NATO, he did not fully perceive the ironic turn which the issue of German rearmament would take with the French proposal of a European army, and the implications of this proposal and of German rearmament itself on American attitudes towards Britain and the Anglo-American Alliance.[22] Nevertheless, Bevin reacted to the American package with caution pending a Cabinet decision, and at the end of the first stage of the talks Acheson reported to President Truman that 'they were prepared to accept what we offered but they were not prepared to accept what we asked. In the situation I am now taking the attitude, not that we are imposing specific conditions, but that we are unable to proceed with the discussion until their attitude is made more clear'.[23] This approach in due course induced the required clarification of attitude, and in December 1950 NATO finally agreed to establish a united command, with General Eisenhower as Supreme Commander, and German rearmament was accepted 'in principle'. But the principle was a far way from the fact, and in the years which elapsed before a framework was finally established for the full participation of Germany in European defence it was the Anglo-American alliance which prevailed as the mainstay of Western defence and the teeth of the Atlantic Alliance. This in turn had serious implications on Britain's attitude to the European movement and on the score of British participation in European defence arrangements.

The supremacy of the Anglo-American alliance until the middle fifties owed itself mainly to the vacuum which for want of German participation continued to exist in the Continental European contribution to Western defence for some five years after the signing of the North Atlantic Treaty, and to the structure of NATO itself. But the actual postwar revival of the alliance cannot be viewed simply as an inevitable occurrence pending the restoration of military strength on the Continent. As a cardinal objective of British foreign policy the revival of the Anglo-American alliance was pursued not only as a means of securing Western Europe, but also as a means of securing Britain from the European movement towards unity by providing the basis for her traditional world role centred around the Commonwealth, Western Europe, and the United States. Moreover, until the early fifties there was a very real Anglo-American interdependence in defence, arising on the American side from the dependence of the United States on air bases in Britain for the delivery of the American atomic capability on the likely target of Moscow, which was at the time beyond the direct reach of the chosen vehicle of delivery, the B-29 bomber. Informal Anglo-American agreement was reached between December 1947 and January 1948 on the location of American bombers in England,[24] and the British Government in offering its prompt and informal consent to the establishment of American bases was all too aware of the impetus which such action would give to the revival of the postwar Anglo-American alliance. But if the Anglo-American Bases Agreement was the first concrete manifestation of the postwar alliance, its revival must also be seen within the broader context of general Anglo-American cooperation in the early postwar years, and in the survival of elements of the wartime alliance. The growth of a joint Anglo-American front in Germany with the creation of Bizonia, in December 1946; the constant political collaboration between the two countries on issues with the Soviet Union; the prima donna role of Britain in the European response to the Marshall Plan were all part of the background of postwar Anglo-American cooperation on which the alliance was gradually able to reconstruct itself. At the same time, there were in the military field the surviving wartime arrangements for standardisation of military equipment and officer training, and agreement for the reinvigoration of the Joint Chiefs of Staff. Even within the abrasive field of atomic energy cooperation, the Combined Policy Committee, established in 1943 by the United States, Britain, and

Canada for joint supervision of the A-bomb development, survived into the postwar years and was responsible for directing the restricted cooperation between the three countries on atomic matters. On another level, there was the psychological basis of the historical Anglo-American relationship,[25] and particularly the continuing close personal Anglo-American leadership ties built up during the war as, for example, between Winston Churchill, General Eisenhower, and General Sir Hastings Ismay, which contributed so much to the revival in the postwar years of the unique Anglo-American alliance. The depth of Anglo-American sentiment surviving the war is fully recorded in the postwar correspondence of these men. 'It is a great joy to me', wrote Churchill to Eisenhower in the critical month of July 1948, when the first set of American bombers were being transferred to East Anglia with the curtain rising on the Berlin Crisis, 'to see our two countries working together ever more closely. In this alone lies the salvation of the world. I feel we shall always be marching together along that road.'[26] And from the other side of the Atlantic, Eisenhower recalls to Ismay that 'one of the great miracles of victory was the partnership of Britain and America. I've tried to live for the development and perpetuation of B-A friendship.'[27] Even though such spontaneous overflow of feeling was largely confined to the commanders who worked so closely together during the war, the influence of such personal relationships on the revival of the Anglo-American alliance cannot easily be overestimated. By 1948 the Anglo-American relationship was increasingly displaying a broad level of cooperation over and above its serious frictions, and with the supreme Anglo-American effort during the Berlin Crisis, the Anglo-American alliance had finally and signally restored itself in a central position within the postwar relations of the Western camp. But the pre-eminence of the Anglo-American alliance was most clearly reflected in the Anglo-American directorate of NATO, which in structure and organisation was an all too obvious expression of the hard fact of Anglo-American cooperation constituting the mainstay of Western security. NATO's Standing Group, for instance, amounted to little more than a revival of the World War II Combined Chiefs of Staff Committee, now with the new addition of France, while SHAPE, which in the event of war would automatically assume full responsibility for all military operations in the European theatre, was in most respects the reincarnation of SHAEF. Not only in structure but in

appointments too, with General Eisenhower as Supreme Allied
Commander of Europe and Lord Ismay as Secretary-General of
NATO and Vice-Chairman of its Council, NATO was fashioned
around the Anglo-American alliance and effectively rested on
Anglo-American power.

Although it was in the sphere of defence that the United States
most consistently viewed Britain as being on a separate footing from
the Continent, there was always the firm belief in Washington
that the relative reduction of Britain's power with the emergence
of the USA and Russia as super-powers could not be counteracted,
and that there would be indeed an inevitable widening of the
gap which would before long place Britain much more on the
continental side of the scale, after the reconstruction of European
defence, than among the super-powers. Besides this, the difficult
problems attendant on the construction of a European defence
system, particularly the perplexing issue of German participation,
together with the diminishing reality of Anglo-American interdependence brought about by developments in nuclear weapons
and changing strategic concepts, gradually impelled the United
States during the fifties to regard Britain as belonging realistically
within a Western European defence framework.

One important element behind this shift in the American attitude was the increasing recognition in Washington that Britain was
quite immovably opposed to being included in schemes for European unity, and the growing American suspicion that she was even
inherently opposed to the evolution of a purely Continental unity,
from which she would by her own desire be excluded. It was
becoming clearer to the United States that Britain was bent on
pursuing her traditional world role and that however indispensable
the Anglo-American alliance was to the West it was increasingly
coming into conflict with the European movement in as much as
its existence belied the postwar realities of Britain's power and
blinded Britain to her role, which the Americans saw as leading,
from within, the movement towards Western European unity as
one pillar in an Atlantic Community. On the British side, however,
NATO's multilateral structure provided a ready-made framework
for the predominance of the Anglo-American alliance, especially
in the absence of a united European defence component. The real
problem as the British saw it was to prevent the growth of such a
disparity of power between the super-powers and Britain, and such
a diminution in the degree of interdependence within the Anglo-

American alliance, as to encourage American beliefs that Britain was destined in the postwar era to be a second-class power whose only salvation lay in European unity. Britain's approach to this problem lay outside NATO in the nuclear field where Britain strove to achieve nuclear status, originally mainly as a matter of defence but increasingly as a means of trying to forge a joint Anglo-American partnership in weapons development and strategy, which more than anything would guarantee the survival of the Anglo-American alliance and ensure Britain a place at summitry.

Anglo-American atomic energy cooperation had developed during the Second World War and despite serious frictions within this field, the Quebec Agreement of 19 August 1943 and the Agreed Declaration of 16 November 1945 constituted an optimistic basis for continued cooperation in the postwar years. The Quebec Agreement between Roosevelt and Churchill stipulated that the principle of 'mutual consent' would govern the use of the atomic bomb, and that there would be effective cooperation between the United States and Britain in the postwar development of atomic energy: the Agreed Declaration was for full collaboration among the United States, Britain and Canada in the atomic field. But Britain's postwar hopes for the evolution of an Anglo-American atomic energy partnership were quite soon shattered by the passage of the United States Atomic Energy Act (McMahon Act) of 1946, which by stringently restricting access to American developments in this field, flew in the face of the two agreements and effectively legislated the termination of the close war-time collaboration between the United States, Britain, and Canada. Months of acrimonious dispute followed in the wake of the McMahon Act, with Britain accusing the United States of gross breach of faith and with strenuous denials issuing from Washington amidst the anti-British, nationalist strains of the American nuclear monopolists on Capitol Hill. This rather unhappy episode eventually subsided with the partial restoration of Anglo-American atomic energy cooperation by the so-called '*modus vivendi*' of 7 January 1948. Under this arrangement Britain was granted access to information in nine areas related to commercial and industrial employment of atomic energy, and agreed in return to relinquish to the United States British uranium supplies from the Congo for 1948, and the bulk of that for 1949. But the *modus vivendi* stopped short of the most vital area of British interest by excluding provisions for any cooperation or exchange of information on weapons development. Nevertheless, while fully recognising the critical limitations of the compromise, the British Government was prone to see the *modus vivendi* as a step in the right direction, as a concession towards further concessions, particularly as the American need for increased accessibility to British controlled uranium supplies and potential Commonwealth resources pointed to a very basic Anglo-American interdependence in the atomic energy field.

Left to the Truman Administration, such a policy of increasing Anglo-American cooperation might have developed more rapidly in the early stages of the Cold War, but any chance of this happening was effectively blocked by the unrelenting opposition of influential voices in Congress and a division within the Atomic Energy Commission. The argument for increasing cooperation rested not only on the degree of Anglo-American interdependence in defence, but on the fact that Britain herself was slowly but determinedly embarking on the nuclear trail. One of the consequences of the disruption of Anglo-American atomic energy cooperation caused by the restrictive policies of the United States, culminating in the McMahon Act, was the stimulation of Britain's national nuclear programme. The United States had indeed been forewarned of this by Clement Attlee, who had assured Averell Harriman that should the McMahon Bill be enacted, then Britain would find it necessary 'to build her own plants for atomic energy production for both military and civil purposes'.[28] In the event, by the autumn of 1946 Britain had embarked on her own programme of weapons development. The overriding consideration at the time was Britain's immediate security, given all the uncertainty surrounding American isolationism. But an interrelated factor was precisely the need not merely to extract from the United States a firm commitment to Britain and Western Europe, but to actually involve the United States in their defence. The belief which gradually took hold in Britain was that the surest way of binding the United States to the defence of Western Europe was in having a controlling hand in American nuclear strategy. This meant in effect Anglo-American nuclear partnership, thought possible only if Britain were to clearly demonstrate to the Americans her ability and intent to join the nuclear race, notwithstanding the McMahon Act.

By 1951, with the recognition that both the United States and the

Soviet Union were making rapid strides as nuclear powers; that increased American troops to Western Europe and an integrated command for NATO had been achieved only under strong European pressure; that German rearmament was not only imminent but might provide the United States with a justification for withdrawing its troops on the Continent, Britain began to attach considerably more weight to her nuclear programme. In January 1951 the British Government allocated the unprecedented peacetime total of £4·7 billion to a three-year rearmament schedule, and in October 1952 Britain successfully tested her first atomic bomb, to be followed five years later by her first hydrogen bomb.

In 1949, with the *modus vivendi* due to expire, the Truman Administration sought to win Congressional support for an extension of the basis of agreement with Britain towards a limited Anglo-American atomic partnership. But in this particularly sensitive area of policy bipartisan support was essential for any such step, and ideas for increasing the scope of Anglo-American atomic collaboration continuously met with powerful opposition from Republican Senators Vandenberg, Hickenlooper, Knowland and Millikin, as well as from Lewis Strauss on the Atomic Energy Commission, and Secretary of Defense Louis Johnson, who was increasingly at odds with the Administration. Their opposition was an equal mixture of Anglophobia and atomic nationalism. Britain was known to be pressing for increased collaboration with the United States, and the British Government had put forward an optimistic programme for partnership which went far beyond even what the Administration was prepared to envisage. In the circumstances, however, nothing could be achieved as there was no chance of putting through Congress the necessary supportive legislation, and the Administration had to shelve its approach in favour of an interim renewal of the *modus vivendi*. At the beginning of 1950, the British security disclosures during the Fuchs affair, by confirming the worst American suspicions of the hazards of information exchanges with Britain, finally eliminated indefinitely any prospect of a more favourable reception in the United States of ideas for full Anglo-American collaboration.

Britain's decision in 1946 to continue the development of her own national nuclear programme, both despite and because of the McMahon Act, handed her an important diplomatic lever during the early fifties. It established beyond doubt the supremacy of the Anglo-American alliance. There were two main features of this—

supremacy within the multilateral conventionally equipped Atlantic
alliance, in terms of an Anglo-American directorate; and, secondly,
exclusive Anglo-American nuclear control and growing partnership outside the Atlantic alliance. Although the Anglo-American
partnership was chiefly at the level of strategic planning and
consultation, and did not include exchange of information on
weapons development, there was extensive cooperation and in the
spring of 1950, Britain's RAF received seventy B-29 bombers
from the United States under the military assistance programme.
These long-range bombers were further equipped with nuclear
weapons provided by the United States. There was also some
coordination between the RAF and America's Strategic Air Command (SAC) and in 1954 the Eisenhower Administration managed
to have Congress amend the Atomic Energy Act of 1946, thereby
allowing the Administration a freer hand in making concessions
to its allies for the proper adaptation of the Atlantic alliance
to the changing nature of strategy. Although the amendments did
not permit of the passing on of 'know how', the new legislation
was nevertheless a step in that direction, and went so far as to
allow the stationing of American nuclear weapons in Western
Europe. The implications of the strengthening of the Anglo-
American alliance on Britain's relations with Western Europe were
profound. The most far-reaching, however, was in the nuclear
strategic aspect of the Anglo-American alliance. Having classed
herself as a nuclear power, Britain could lay concrete and justifiable claim to being in a fundamentally different position from
the continental countries, as much in terms of power as of world-
wide commitments, and Britain on that ground was able to resist
being any more involved in Western Europe and European unity
than the United States itself. By the end of 1950, the main priori-
ties of Britain concerning the United States and Western Europe
had been achieved—American commitment to and involvement
in the defence of Western Europe under the North Atlantic Treaty,
the establishment of an organisation for the execution of the
treaty, and the steady progress toward Anglo-American collaboration at the level of nuclear strategy. But above all, the British
Government had ensured the paramountcy of the Anglo-American
alliance while also proposing an alternative framework to European unity in the form of the mulilateral Atlanticist regional
concept of NATO. For its part, the United States had made little
headway in getting the Europeans to accept the formula of unity,

least of all in reorientating Britain's perspective from Common-wealth to Europe. The position at the beginning of 1950 was that the United States still faced the problem with which it had begun, the postwar organisation of Western Europe towards regional unity under British leadership. Preoccupation with the military aspects of containment, participation in the North Atlantic Treaty Organisation, generally *ad hoc* responsive policies in the critical postwar period, a conflict in American policy between short-run necessities and long-term goals, were all among the chief factors on the American side which favoured British diplomacy during the formative period of United States policy.

5

The Schuman Plan

The year 1950 marked a significant turning point for American attitudes concerning Britain's relations with Western Europe. The basic feature of this shift was the new tendency of the United States to acquiesce fully in Britain's chosen international role of close liaison with the Commonwealth, the United States and the countries of Western Europe, and for the United States to look elsewhere than to Britain for leadership towards Western European unity. Hand in hand with the need for the Anglo-American alliance and the recognition of British influence on the Continent, this new attitude viewed Britain as a bridge between the United States and continental Western Europe. In comparison to the tentative period from 1947 to 1950, American attitudes and policies towards Britain in the six years from 1950 were far more definite and consistent. The shift in attitude owed itself mainly to the emergence of the supranational European movement on the Continent and the initial British response to it in the context of the Schuman Plan.

The Schuman Plan for the establishment of a supranational European Coal and Steel Community was the French corollary to the re-emergence of a German state. The short-lived discordant Four-Power collaboration over Germany had been doomed from the very outset by the supreme interest which each of the powers had in ensuring that the future of Germany fitted entirely into its own conceptions, and from the unbridgeable divergences between the Western powers, on the one hand, and Russia—the most fundamental difference being related to the meaning of the term 'democracy'. It was the basic axiom of all parties concerned that whoever controlled Germany controlled Europe, and none intended to see any of the others do so. The collapse of the Council of Foreign Ministers' meeting in December 1947 finally put an end to the diplomatic masquerade of collaboration, and thereafter the Western powers no longer sought to disguise their primary interest in incorporating the industrial potential of Western Germany into the West, particularly in the interest of the economic recovery and security of Western Europe for which the United States had already promised the premium of Marshall Aid. The Western powers were content to accept the permanent division of Germany as a *fait accompli,* and all tended to see a divided Germany offering more advantages than a united one. France, which had thrice in seventy years been invaded by Germany, adamantly opposed German reunification and reconstruction. At successive Councils of Foreign Ministers from the beginning of 1946, and at meetings of the Western allied occupying powers, the French, looking to their future security, consistently and vigorously de-manded partition from Germany of her main industrial areas— calling for the internationalisation of the Ruhr, political detach-ment and permanent military occupation of the Rhineland, and French control of the Saar. Throughout its term of office, the British Labour Government regarded Germany far more as a potential danger than a potential ally in the rebuilding of Western Europe (Bevin by 1948 was 'trying to steer a middle course'), and there was considerable opposition within the Cabinet to German unity.[1] At the same time, both Britain and the United States were opposed to Russian suggestions for military withdrawal and German reunification under a strong centralised government, in the fear that such a German state might fall to Russia either through military invasion,[2] or even, perhaps, through democratic processes. In the following passage from a memorandum of a conversation between Acheson and Dulles, the latter described the nature of the dilemma which the United States faced in Russian proposals for a reunited centralised Germany:

At the London Council of Foreign Ministers [November to Dec-ember 1947] the Soviet had exposed its intention to get control of all of Germany and thereby to dominate the rest of the Continent. In pursuance of this policy, Soviet propaganda actively advocates that Germany should be reunited and returned to the Germans, that the military occupation be ended, and that a central government be re-established at Berlin. The Russians felt that they had developed and organized eastern Germany and had penetrated political and labor organizations in Western Germany to such a degree that if their German solution were adopted, they would dominate Germany. They also believed that if their solution were rejected by the Western

Allies and the division and occupation prolonged, this would be so
displeasing to all Germans that they would then turn towards the
Soviets as allies, so that this also would enable the Soviets to undermine the influence in Germany of the West.

As the situation was when the Atlantic Pact began to be discussed,
and as it still is, a withdrawal of United States occupation troops
from Germany or the segregation of such troops in isolated areas
such as Bremen and Hamburg and the establishment of a central
all-German government would raise very serious problems. The
American troops are now a barrier between the Red Armies and
Western Europe, they help to divide Germany and they form a vital
part of the government of Germany. Withdrawal of that barrier and
ending of the division of Germany and its military government
would so accentuate fear of Russia, plus Germany, that fear, not
confidence, would become the dominating force in Western Europe.
Serious political division between the Western Allies would be inevitable, a French internal crisis would be probable with, perhaps,
civil war between communists and de Gaullists. Therefore, under
present conditions, if the United States had to face up to the problem
of Germany as a whole, it would probably not be able to accept
a reuniting of Germany and ending of military occupation and
government. We would be almost forced to adopt a negative attitude
which is not [sic] solution and which would throw the Germans and
the Russians together.

Temporarily, the Soviet blockade of West Berlin spares the Western
Powers the necessity of facing up to the problem of Germany as a
whole.[3]

Following the fiasco of the Council of Foreign Ministers in
December 1947, the United States and Britain, with reluctant
French support, rapidly developed a programme for rebuilding
Western Germany and allying it to the West. American and
British agreement on 20 February 1948 to the virtually accom-
plished fact of the incorporation of the Saar by the French
economy was part of the initial price paid for French acquiescence
in the Anglo-American plans for the reconstruction of Western
Germany. Three days later, on 23 February, the first stage of
discussions among the three Western occupying powers and the
Benelux countries, who had been requested to attend, began in
London on the restoration of Western Germany. By the end of the
second stage of the talks, in June, substantial agreement had been
reached by the participants on the London Programme.[4] France
was further appeased by agreement on international control of the
Ruhr by the six powers, and that Western Germany would not

have a place on the envisaged International Authority until a German federal constitution came into being. The Ruhr Statute was adopted on 28 December 1948, and the Authority was created on 28 April 1949. The London Programme itself had successfully reduced the problem of Germany to that of constituting some seemingly legitimate West German political authority preparatory to the full incorporation of Western Germany into the West, for the utilisation of its economic and military potential in the service of Western strength and security. The view held from immediately after the war that Germany must be made to pay her own way was extended in September 1947, as a prelude to the inclusion of the Western zones of Germany in the European Recovery Programme, to the conviction that 'if European recovery is to be effective the German economy must be fitted into the European economy so that it may contribute to a general improvement in the standard of living'.[5] Now with agreement, in June 1948, on the London Programme the political as well as the economic revival of Germany were well under way. The Berlin blockade imposed by the Russians from 22 June 1948 until 12 May 1949, ostensibly over the currency reforms being carried out in the Western sectors of Germany, merely increased the determination of the United States and Britain to implement the London Programme for the constitution of a West German state.[6] The Council of Foreign Ministers' meeting of 23 May 1949, was agreed to out of mutual interest in ending the blockade and counter-blockade,[7] and provided the Western powers with the opportunity of serving formal notice to the Soviet Union of their intention to proceed on the basis of the London Programme for dealing with Western Germany.[8] Accordingly, after the promulgation of the Occupation Statute and the Basic Law in May, elections were held in August, then the termination of military government, and the entry into force of the Occupation Statute of 21 September 1949, signalled the end of the first stage in the transition of Western Germany to full sovereignty within the European community and the Western bloc. At the Paris Foreign Ministers' Conference, between 9 and 10 November, further discussion was already taking place on the final steps in the rapid progress towards complete German sovereignty.[9] Among the important issues considered were the termination of the Occupation Statute, the ending of the state of war, the removal of the four-power agreement restricting German shipbuilding, establishment of German direct diplomatic representation, as well as German participation in international organisations and in the Council of Europe. By the end of 1949, therefore, a reconstituted sovereign state of Western Germany was an immediate prospect for Europe.

The main obstacle to the Anglo-American policy of reconstructing Western Germany as a sovereign state was the anxiety of France. Although substantial concessions had been made in an effort to reduce French fears of a revival of German militarism, none of the safeguards and assurances could bring the French to readily accommodate themselves to the reconstitution of Western Germany less than five years after the war. A major French concern was still the future of the Ruhr. The German Federal Republic had acceded to the High Authority in November 1949 and there was the very real possibility that the Authority might develop a policy more in line with Germany's wishes than with France's, and that the industrial-military potential of Germany might at some stage be re-created. To aggravate this pressing issue, France had not only to face the economic and political revival of its historical enemy, but was confronted with the impending rearmament of the Germans. The possibility of German rearmament, the main point of Anglo-American divergence over German reconstruction, had been under consideration in the United States from the spring of 1949,[10] and by the end of that year, following the establishment of the German Federal Republic, German rearmament was gaining control of the Truman Administration's thinking and there was increasing discussion of the subject on both sides of the Atlantic.[11]

Against this background, there was from the end of 1949 a pronounced awareness of the immediate necessity of a permanent Franco-German *modus vivendi*. This was appreciated by none so much as the French and Germans. Continued conflicts, particularly over the Saar in January 1950, merely served to underline for the French this pressing need for an enduring solution to the problem of Germany. At the same time, Chancellor Adenauer had been showing himself increasingly anxious to placate French fears in order that Germany might regain equal status with her Western European neighbours. The idea of pooling the European coal and steel industries, which had been mooted time and again over the years,[12] was frequently discussed from late 1949, particularly in terms of extending the area of control of the Ruhr Authority, as a means of eliminating French fears of a revival of German industrial-military potential. In November 1949, Adenauer put forward general suggestions to the French Government for French investment of up to forty per cent in German industries as a means of meeting French demands for security,[13] and in his talks on the Saar with French Foreign Minister Schuman, in January 1950, the German Chancellor further indicated his sincere interests in any proposals for some mutually acceptable accommodation between the two countries. For France the circumstances were altogether compelling, given the clear American intention of reconstituting and rearming Western Germany, and also the new turn in the East-West balance arising from the recently acquired atomic capability of the Soviet Union. The dramatic French response was the Schuman Plan which signified an historic shift in French policy and cleared the way for a lasting Franco-German rapprochement.

On 9 May 1950, appropriately enough on the eve of the London Foreign Ministers' Conference in which Germany was the main subject, M. Schuman announced the revolutionary proposal for a Franco-German coal-steel pool 'under a common High Authority, in an organisation open to the participation of other countries of Europe'.[14] According to Schuman himself, the purpose of his proposal 'was not economic but eminently political. ... If an organisation such as he was proposing were to be set up, it would enable each country to detect the first signs of rearmament, and would have an extraordinarily calming effect in France.'[15] The chief intellectual inspiration behind the Schuman Plan was, however, the renowned Europeanist Jean Monnet,[16] and naturally enough the long-term attraction of the proposal lay in its conception of a supranational coal and steel community as 'the first step in the Federation of Europe'.[17] From the standpoint of the United States, therefore, the Schuman Plan contained within it the twin advantages of paving the way for the success of America's German policy, and of providing a bold concrete step towards the implementation of the United States long-term conception of European unity. The first foreign statesman to have been informed of the Schuman Plan was Secretary of State Acheson. On 8 May during a brief visit to Paris en route to London, Acheson was introduced to the French proposal by Schuman in the presence of Monnet. The immediate reaction of the Secretary of State was one of stunned incredulity. It took him some time to accept that the two Frenchmen were serious, and to overcome his initial suspicions

about the plan being simply a guise for a cartel. Once convinced
about the sincerity of French intentions, however, Acheson gave
his complete and unequivocal support to the proposal, and forth-
with wired President Truman informing him of the revolution
about to occur and bidding him do nothing until further notice.
When, therefore, the Schuman Plan was dramatically announced
on the following evening, the French already knew that it was
blessed with American support. They also knew that Chancellor
Adenauer, who had been informed on 9 May, 'wholeheartedly'
accepted the French proposal.[18] The reactions of the other Western
European countries remained in the balance. But inasmuch as the
Schuman Plan was conceived primarily in relation to France and
Germany, the French were assured of the success of the plan, with
whatever American support was necessary, even before it was
publicly announced.[19]

By the end of May, the Benelux countries and Italy had
indicated their acceptance of the supranational principle behind
the Schuman Plan, and their willingness to participate in negotiations on the proposal. The reaction of Britain to the news of the
French proposal which it received on 9 May was, however, far
less cooperative. To fully comprehend the nature of the British
response to the Schuman proposal, one must see it in the broad
context of the objectives of British foreign policy from 1947.[20]
The focal point of British opposition to the Schuman Plan was
the supranational question. But this really involved two issues.
The first was the supranational formula *per se,* and the second
was the stipulation that it should be accepted in principle as a
pre-condition to participation in the negotiations. The latter was
the immediate battle-ground between Britain and France, with the
French seeing it as the fundamental inviolable permanent guarantee of their future security against Germany, while the British
wanted it waived in order that Britain might enter the negotiations
to negotiate away the supranational formula. The French had
stipulated prior acceptance of the supranational principle precisely
to avert any such eventuality, and the plan was the principle. In
the unheralded dramatic announcement of the Schuman proposal,
the British were thus faced with a major diplomatic coup and
accomplished fact of Franco-German agreement, endorsed by
the United States, for which they had been entirely unprepared.[21]
The initial quarrel of the British Government over protocol relating to the manner and timing of the French proposal, shortly

before the Foreign Ministers' Conference, really indicated their profound exasperation with being put on the spot for a 'yes' or 'no' answer to the supranational principle already accepted by France and Germany, and the likelihood of it being agreed to by other continental countries. Bevin's policy of building Western Union as a close association of sovereign European states linked to the Commonwealth, and supported by the United States within an Atlanticist framework, had been remarkably successful in the three years between 5 June 1947 and 9 May 1950. During this time, the British Government had resisted American and European interest in European unity by taking the initiatives and cooperating in the European movement, while ensuring that it stopped within the limits of the closest possible inter-governmental cooperation short of unity. The significance of the Schuman Plan for Britain was that it threatened to undermine the whole progress of the Labour Government's foreign policy, and not simply that it entailed some relinquishing of British sovereignty for participation. Not only was Britain's paramountcy in Western Europe being challenged by France, but in actively assisting the reconstruction of Germany and hoping for Franco-German reconciliation, the very last thing the British Government was trying to do was to make a Franco-German rapprochement the nucleus for a continental unity. This is what the Schuman Plan seemed to offer, and to this extent, apart from counteracting the ends of British diplomacy, it conjured up the old Napoleonic spectre.

Bevin was informed of the Schuman Plan by the French Ambassador, M. Massigli, on 9 May between sessions of Anglo-American discussions with Secretary of State Acheson.[22] Acheson tried in vain to impress upon Bevin that the Schuman Plan presented a boat which Britain could ill afford to miss. But the British Foreign Secretary, provoked by the eleventh-hour disclosure of the plan to Britain, and now aware of Acheson's earlier knowledge during his tête-à-tête with Schuman and Monnet in Paris, plus being already aggravated by allegedly 'inspired' American press criticism of British 'foot-dragging' on the matter of European unity,[23] was quite convinced that the Schuman Plan was an American-French conspiracy, and there developed a serious rift between the two statesmen.[24] Bevin himself was only too aware that the terms in which negotiations on the Schuman Plan were proposed raised the immediate possibility of the European movement either running away from or running away with Britain.

G

Britain was being forced to unequivocally declare for or against European unity. The British Government had not the slightest intention of accepting the supranational principle. When it had recovered from the initial shock of France's sudden diplomacy, the hope of the British Government was that it could get the French to withdraw their stipulation. On 3 June the last of successive British attempts to win acceptance of an alternative basis for negotiations was rejected by the Six, leaving the British Government to deeply regret that 'it was impossible in view of their responsibility to Parliament and people to associate themselves with the negotiations on the terms proposed by the French Government'.[25] Thereafter, it was the British hope that the negotiations would fail, or that even if they did succeed it would be possible to find some sort of arrangement with the community which would re-establish the course of British policy. In April 1951 the treaty establishing the European Coal and Steel Community was signed in Paris, and it came into operation on 25 July 1952. Two years later, in December 1954, a consultative agreement was reached between Britain and the ECSC, but by that time the European movement had somewhat swung itself back in Britain's favour.

Owing to the overwhelming popular acclaim accorded to the Schuman Plan as the most far-reaching initiative towards European unity, Britain's rejection of the offer to participate in the negotiations naturally exposed her to very unfavourable criticism from the American public. It was generally accepted that despite her professed genuine interest in the proposal, Britain's rejection of the supranational principle was a deliberate blow at the very core of the 'European' idea. Moreover, the general irritation with the British stand on the Schuman Plan was given a high emotional charge by the untimely publication, on 13 June, of the Labour Party's pamphlet 'European Unity'.[26] Drawn up by the Labour Party's National Executive, the pamphlet advocated a strong Socialist foreign policy, rejected the supranational concept, and denounced British participation in any schemes for European economic and political unity. As American opinion wedded the Government's attitude to the Schuman Plan to the views expressed in the pamphlet, the result was a spontaneous fury and torrent of criticism to the extent that Washington had to pressure the Labour Government into publicly dissociating itself from the pamphlet.[27] Notwithstanding Attlee's embarrassment over the timing of the publication and its hostile reception, 'European Unity' had in fact been 'unanimously approved after a short discussion' at a meeting of the Labour Party's National Executive Council, on 24 May, at which Attlee, Bevin, Cripps, Dalton, and Herbert Morrison were all present.[28] In the deluge of American criticism about the pamphlet, Britain was attacked on practically every conceivable ground,[29] and there was even a demand from some Republican Senators that Britain be 'fined' $340 million in aid cuts until she joined the Schuman Plan.[30] Despite the drama occasioned by the Labour Party pamphlet, there were, however, some more reasoned American judgements on Britain's attitude to the Schuman Plan. The Washington correspondent for the *Yorkshire Post* commented on the feeling in America that Britain preferred 'to hamper [European] integration by slow sabotage',[31] and according to Harold Callender:

The view here is that the British would have been more candid and on firmer ground if they had frankly said that their planned economy and their Commonwealth relations had prevented their joining the Schuman plan, instead of saying that they sought constructive action while declining any commitments to the action proposed.

The view is growing on the Continent that the British Government not only is reluctant to take part in uniting Europe but, in conformity with the traditional balance-of-power practices, actually dislikes the idea of a strong united Continent.[32]

But it was Senator J. W. Fulbright, ranking member of the Foreign Relations Committee and one of the chief proponents of European unity, who in his plaintive warning to Britain most fully represented the sentiment of America. In addressing the Senate, he noted that:

... with regard to practically all other suggestions concerning European unification, the present Labour Government of Great Britain has been reluctant to lend its support. I sincerely hope that in this instance that government will consider most seriously the possible consequences of rebuffing this courageous and far-sighted leadership on the part of the French Government.

Many of us, including myself, have been losing our enthusiasm for the Marshall Plan because of the apparent impossibility of making any progress towards European federation. If none is made, I believe the British must assume much of the responsibility, and I believe the consequences will be very serious indeed.[33]

The public attitude of the Truman Administration towards Britain's rejection of the offer to participate in negotiations on the Schuman Plan was diplomatically non-committal. The State Department is reported to have found it 'a source of satisfaction to know that the Government of the United Kingdom, although it feels unable to accept in advance of further exploration the far-reaching implications of the French proposal, has expressed sympathy with the broad purposes of the Schuman plan and has stated the hope that the plan will work out in such a way as to permit British participation'.[34] According to the *New York Times,* 'if Britain's requirements at home, in the Commonwealth and the sterling area make it unwise or politically impractical for the British to give up their sovereignty over their coal and steel industries, United States officials will understand that decision'.[35] Secretary of State Acheson, in testimony before the House Foreign Affairs Committee, commented that he did not consider there was a British 'refusal' to join the negotiations on the Schuman Plan, but only a disagreement about the time at which Britain should become involved; he himself, he said, was 'neither dismayed nor discouraged' by the British action.[36]

The Schuman Plan was seen by the Truman Administration as being first of all a magnificent opportunity for the fulfilment of its German policy. Conspicuously enough, the signing of the ECSC treaty in April 1951 was followed on 26 May 1952 by the signing of the Bonn Agreements restoring German sovereignty, and the signature of the EDC treaty on the next day. Particularly from the viewpoint of a Franco-German rapprochement allaying French fears of Germany, and facilitating swift unimpeded completion of the process of German reconstitution within the West, the overriding concern of Secretary Acheson was quite simply that the Schuman Plan should succeed, and succeed as soon as possible. The Secretary of State indeed hoped for and would certainly have welcomed British participation in the negotiations. But at the same time that he could hardly expect British participation on account of the supranational stipulation, he well realised that British participation without prior acceptance of the supranational principle would be courting defeat of the Schuman Plan, at least in its most important aspect, not only for French security but for the general cause of European unity.[37] These advantages were far too important and urgent for the United States to risk the possibility of a watered-down international agreement eventually replacing the original version of the plan, merely in order to enlarge its membership to include Britain:

> The United States Government has no confidence an international coal and steel board, with limited powers to recommend and advise member governments, would change anything in Europe, and the fear is that this is the kind of limited organization the British would prefer.[38]

First the German, then the Benelux responses to the Schuman Plan presented every possibility of its success without Britain. It was only necessary to ensure that agreement was reached quickly before any doubts were raised by any of the parties. For the United States to become involved in the argument over the stipulation of prior acceptance of the supranational principle would have merely delayed a process which seemed almost ready made, induced accusations of taking sides, and encouraged suspicions that the plan originated in Washington. Once final agreement was reached and the proposed ECSC established, there would be nothing to prevent Britain joining, and indeed Britain might be forced to under pressure of continental economic competition. With such considerations, there was certainly little reason to be either 'dismayed' or 'discouraged' about Britain's refusal.

What the Truman Administration hoped, was that even though Britain could not bring herself to accept the supranational principle, she would play a full supportive role, giving her utmost encouragement and using all her influence to make the plan succeed. The Administration still tended to think that while Britain was hesitant about European unity for herself, she nevertheless supported it for the Continent. Consequently, the main annoyance of the Administration with Britain was not that she refused to participate in the negotiations, but derived from the Administration's impression that Britain was placing far too much emphasis on the negative aspects of her relationship with the proposal and not at all encouraging its success. Hence the self-restraining critical attitude towards Britain which showed itself throughout the entire negotiations, and the effort of the Administration to extract some gesture of support from Britain for the ECSC proposal. For although the Administration was quite confident that British participation was not necessary and would most likely be detrimental to the realisation of the Schuman plan as a supranational community, it was far less certain that Continental agreement would be reached, and reached quickly, if Britain did not give maximum encouragement while remaining aloof. Especially towards the end of 1951, when the Truman Administration had come to link the ratification of the ECSC treaty with the success of the EDC, it was particularly anxious that the British Government, now under the Conservatives, would correct its predecessor's posture and give forthright support to both schemes. The Administration's attitude then is quite accurately revealed in the following extract:

United States officials hope that during his visit to President Truman in Washington in January, Prime Minister Churchill will take publicly a more positive attitude toward the Schuman Plan for pooling coal and steel production and the European army project than British leaders have taken hitherto.

It is believed that if the Prime Minister should give to the two measures for European unity a more definite British endorsement, the outlook for the two projects would be improved.

It is understood a clearer expression of approval of the two measures may be urged upon Mr. Churchill by W. Averell Harriman, Director of the Mutual Security Agency, on an early visit to London that will precede his return to Washington. . . .

United States officials do not suggest that Britain should join in the Schuman plan, the European army or any other project looking to a European federation. They accept the often-reiterated British refusal to participate in any form of European unity that entails supranational institutions. But they contend that, even though the British remain out of the coal and steel pool and the European army, they might facilitate the success of these projects by approving and encouraging them.[39]

Both the Schuman Plan and the British response to it had profound implications on American attitudes and policies towards Britain's relations with Western Europe. On the one hand, the United States was presented with a dynamic proposal as a major step in the functional approach towards Western European unity: on the other hand, the Truman Administration, which had consistently looked to Britain for leadership within the European movement, was faced with Britain's polite self-exclusion from negotiations on the French proposal. Certain significant inferences were drawn from this situation. Most important was that the French proposal and its enthusiastic Continental response served to convince the Administration that the Continental countries were prepared to move faster and farther towards European unity than was Britain. The Continentals were clearly capable of taking major initiatives on their own, and it followed that British leadership in the European movement was not as necessary as it had been assumed to be by the Administration in the three years before the Schuman Plan was proposed. After the British rejection of the offer to negotiate on the Schuman Plan, the residual hope that Britain might subsequently reverse her position, particularly with the return of the Conservatives to power, was quite soon dashed. For the Conservative Government, formed in October 1951, immediately made it quite clear in relation to both the ECSC and the EDC that they themselves had no intention whatsoever of sacrificing their sovereignty on the altar of European unity. In the view of a high-ranking official in the State Department, 'the Conservatives were even worse on Europe than Labour, and Eden thought he was a Palmerston'.

The Schuman Plan had thus pointed to the practicability of proceeding along the functional path towards a purely Continental unity, based on a Franco-German nucleus and initially comprising the Six. A Continental unity, however, much less a smaller unity of the Six, was never regarded as the final objective of United States policy. That remained a unity of Western Europe including Britain. But given the attitude of Britain on participation in European unity, and the sympathetic Scandinavian support for it which was so clearly demonstrated at, for instance, the Conference of Strasbourg in November 1951,[40] it was naturally considered desirable and necessary to encourage whatever progress could be made by the Six, even if others did not want to join. Before the Schuman Plan, European unity was only a long-term aim of the United States, and between 1947 and 1950 the Truman Administration was mainly concerned with recovery in Western Europe through economic integration. The effect of the Schuman Plan was not only to make possible a major degree of genuine economic integration in vital areas, but, in the concept of the High Authority, to present a decisive step towards supranational political unity. By the end of 1950, United States policy towards Western Europe had evolved from its formative stage and was taking a definite position. If the Schuman Plan in May placed European unity on the horizon, the Korean War which erupted in June brought added urgency to American interest in German rearmament and the permanent consolidation of Western Europe. The second French proposal, by Premier René Pleven in October 1950, for a European Defence Community seemed to provide an acceptable solution for getting a German contribution to Western defence, and gave further impetus to the European movement on all fronts. Although the Administration never became as wildly optimistic as some of the ardent 'Europeanists' in America who began to see a United States of Europe emerging in the middle fifties, it did shift its focus to place considerably more emphasis on attaining European unity. Accordingly, from 1950 to 1954 American policy in Western Europe was almost exclusively concerned with trying to ensure the swift realisation of the two French proposals, both as ends in themselves and as decisive measures towards European unity. During these crucial years, the United States adopted a fairly constant position on Britain's role in relation to Western Europe, and managed to rationalise some of the earlier ambivalencies in its policies. There was a noticeable acquiescence in Britain's preferred relationship of close cooperation with Western Europe, and a marked tendency towards the so-called 'three-pillar' concept of Atlantic community, which accorded with British policy. Britain was treated simply as a bridge to continental Western Europe, with the recognition that pressure on Britain to correct her self-image and go into Europe might be quite counter-productive, both in relation to European unity and to necessary Anglo-American cooperation. Yet, the essentially *laissez-faire* approach towards Britain, and the attitude that she might be more useful as an instrument for American policy, particularly with respect to continental acceptance of the EDC, was never adopted as a permanent position, and the United States continued to view Britain's postwar role as being ultimately in a unity of Western Europe.

Britain as a 'Bridge': the EDC episode

Less than six months after the French proposal for a European Coal and Steel Community, the French Prime Minister, René Pleven, attempted to advance the supranational European movement one stage farther. On 24 October 1950, he proposed the creation of a European Defence Community, in which German contingents would be fully integrated with those from other participating countries under a single integrated supranational command.[1] The idea of a European Army had earlier been suggested by Winston Churchill, in August, before the Consultative Assembly of the Council of Europe, and Churchill even accepted an amendment by the Assembly calling for a European Minister of Defence. While grave doubt is naturally cast upon the seriousness of Churchill's proposal for a European Army within which 'we would all bear a worthy and honourable part',[2] by his subsequent attitude to the question of British participation in the EDC, it must have seemed to the French a reassuring background for their own proposal two months later. Like the Schuman Plan, the Pleven proposal was a desperate attempt to cope with the problem of Germany. From the outbreak of the Korean War in June 1950, and the accompanying increase in fears of a Russian assault in Western Europe, there was increasing United States pressure for German rearmament. One month before the Pleven proposal, at the New York Tripartite Talks in September, the issue of German rearmament was being heavily pressed by Secretary Acheson on Foreign Ministers Bevin and Schuman.[3]

At the Brussels Foreign Ministers' Conference in December 1950, it was agreed following the Tripartite acceptance of the 'principle', that German participation in Western defence was indispensable. But at Brussels the issue of whether the German contribution should be directly within NATO or by way of the proposed European Defence Community was left open. The American response to the Pleven proposal had been initially quite sceptical. The pressing urgency of a German contribution was the main consideration, and it seemed doubtful whether agreement on the EDC could be reached quickly enough, if at all, to meet the targets of Western defence planning. Nevertheless, during his visit to Washington in December 1950, Pleven had apparently managed to win a concession from the Truman Administration allowing postponement of a final decision on the form of a German contribution pending the forthcoming negotiations on the EDC.[4] On 15 February 1951, the conference on the EDC began in Paris among France, Belgium, Italy, Luxembourg, and the German Federal Republic; while Britain, the United States, the Netherlands, Denmark, Norway, Portugal and Canada were present as observers. At the same time, discussions were being held in Bonn between the three Western High Commissioners and the Adenauer Government on the possibility of a direct German contribution to NATO, which both the United States and Britain tended to favour. The French, however, were adamantly opposed to the inclusion of German units within NATO, and a resolution to this effect was passed a year later, in February 1952, by the French National Assembly, which argued among other things that as the Federal Republic laid claim to other territories, its entry into NATO would change the essentially defensive orientation of the organisation.[5] That apart, both the French and the British were anxious to make decisions regarding German entry into the system of Western defence await the convening of a Four Power conference, called for by the Russians in November 1950, in order that they might have a more definite indication of future Russian attitudes and intentions in its relations with the West. For these reasons, along with other technical difficulties arising from German demands for 'effective reinforcements of Allied troops in Germany' as an indispensable pre-condition to a German defence contribution,[6] and an increasing American enthusiasm for the EDC proposal after the signing of the ECSC Treaty in April 1951, the discussions in Bonn on a direct German contribution to NATO ended without agreement. On the other hand, however, gradual progress was being made in Paris on the EDC proposal. Despite the initial scepticism of the Truman Administration towards the EDC, Acheson had given an American blessing to the opening of the Pleven Conference in Paris, 'emphatically underlining the

positive American attitude'.[7] The Secretary of State is reported
as having written to Foreign Minister Schuman that,

> if the French Government, in the spirit which spoke so distinctly
> from the Schuman Plan, worked out the main outlines of a plan to
> promote the further rapprochement of the free peoples of Europe in
> close contact with the Governments of Germany and the other
> European countries prepared to participate in the common work, one
> was justified in the hopes that long-term solutions for many of the
> present political, economic and military problems might be found.

and he went on to stress that 'the United States Administration
gave its full and wholehearted support to European integration'.[8]
Towards the end of June, substantial agreement was being reached
in the Pleven Plan Conference, and on 24 July 1951, the Conference approved an interim report in which the application of the
supranational principle to the proposed European Defence Community was accepted.[9] From this point the Truman Administration
looked to the EDC as the dual highway for German participation
in Western defence and, taken in conjunction with the ECSC, as
the penultimate step towards European unity among the Six. The
treaty establishing the European Defence Community, together
with protocols making reciprocal guarantees between the EDC
and NATO, were signed by the Six on 27 May 1952, and it was
the hope of the Truman Administration that ratification would
take place 'toward the end of 1952',[10] no doubt before the
scheduled Presidential election.

With the Pleven proposal following so closely on the British
refusal to accept the supranational principle and to participate in
the negotiations on the Schuman Plan, there was little expectation
by the Truman Administration that Britain would be willing to
even contemplate joining the EDC. In the event, the British Labour
Government lost no time in making it quite clear that it could
never see its way to participation in any such venture. Britain's
proposed relationship with the two French proposals, for the
ECSC and the EDC, was carefully expressed in the joint Three
Power Washington Declaration of 14 September 1951, which
declared that 'the Government of the United Kingdom desire to
establish the closest possible association with a European continental community at all stages of its development....'[11] Nevertheless, on the return of the Conservative Government to power in
October 1951, the Truman Administration momentarily 'in-

clined to favour' British participation in the EDC.[12] The Conservatives, however, were no less indisposed than were their pre-
decessors to joining the EDC and European federation; such a
step, according to Eden, ran counter to their instincts, and it was
'something which we know in our bones we cannot do'.[13] As far
as the EDC was concerned, Eden 'feared that the plan, imagina-
tive as it was, might fail for just that reason. It seemed to attempt
too much ...' and he awaited the opportunity to work out 'a more
modest scheme ... without elaborate political superstructure'.[14]
Churchill disliked 'the sludgy amalgam' of EDC—mixing races in
companies if not in platoons—and Eisenhower recalls having used
'every resource at my command, including argument, cajolery, and
sheer prayer, to get Winston to say a single kind word about
EDC'.[15]

American attitudes regarding Britain's relations with the EDC
were quite ambivalent. The EDC, as the second and crucial step
in the supranational movement, embodied the crux of the
American dilemma over Britain's role. From the political standpoint, the EDC symbolised another major progression towards
Western European federation: from the military-strategic perspective, it was a design for securing German participation in Western
European defence, and was itself the contemplated permanent,
fundamental structure of that defence. According to Robert
Schuman, in addressing the Paris Conference:

The Atlantic system may answer and satisfy urgent yet passing
needs ; the problem of Europe persists. We hold the view that regard-
less of the situation of the moment and of any inter-continental or
global solutions found elsewhere, a Europe must be organised, a
Europe that must be redeemed from an anachronistic and absurd
dismemberment, a Europe that must overcome an obsolete nationalism. We have recognised and we proclaim this truth in the field of
economics and of politics. It holds as well for the organisation of
defence if one speaks of a military system intended to last.

Atlantic defence and European defence thus do not exclude each
other and do not cut across each other. They occupy different
planes.[16]

This statement by Schuman is a very important one. Underlying
it is the fact that what the EDC proposal did was to recreate in its
original form the perplexing question of the structure and organisation of Western defence. This was thought to have been substantially solved, at least theoretically with the exception only of

German rearmament, by the establishment of the North Atlantic Treaty Organisation. The question of the artificiality of the regional pact, and the controversy over the concept of a 'dumb-bell' Atlantic community[17] were reintroduced by implication in the EDC episode, and above all it emerged fully that Britain as much as Germany was the central problem in the organisation of Western Europe within an Atlantic framework.

While there was complete agreement within the Truman Administration that Britain's place was ultimately in a united Western Europe, there was far less inclination for immediate British participation in the EDC. The main problem was reconciling the need for Britain's world role, the necessity of the Anglo-American alliance and Britain's central position in NATO, with British participation in a supranational EDC. If Britain joined the EDC, then the 'dumb-bell' conception of Atlantic community which was the end of the Truman policy would be virtually realised; but, on the other hand, there could be no guarantee that the supranational defence community would be willing to divert any degree of its attention from Europe in order to preserve the outskirts of the world from international Communism, as Britain in an independent role could do through her global connections. NATO, which was the framework of the Atlantic community, was after all primarily restricted to Atlantic defence, which would be the limit of the obligations of an EDC within it. An additional consideration of major significance was the development of an independent British nuclear deterrent, which not only underlined the distinction between Britain and the continental powers, but which if placed at the disposal of a supranational community might encourage Third Force and neutralist tendencies already much in evidence in Western Europe. Although the British refusal to participate in the EDC relegated these issues to the background of American thinking on the subject, the problems nevertheless all reappeared at a later date, in the sixties, under different stimuli. Moreover, had the United States fully appreciated the ends of the Labour Government's policy, it might have seen in the EDC the supranational reincarnation of Bevin's Western Union, with an extended membership: and if the United States had looked more carefully at French policy, it might have equally realised that Schuman was looking to the long-term future of a united Europe, and that in building Europe and European defence he was already constructing on a level above the Atlantic community—to his mind 'they occupy different planes'.

The optimistic forecast of the Truman Administration for the ratification of the EDC by the end of 1952 was largely based on the progress of the Six towards the ECSC. The Administration had disappointedly acquiesced in Britain's refusal to negotiate on the Schuman Plan, but was nevertheless quite confident that, provided they had full encouragement from Britain and the United States, the Six would take the leap on their own. This was proving to be the case, and the same reasoning was applied by the Administration to the EDC. But there was a significant difference. Not only Britain's attitude towards the ECSC and the EDC, but, in the case of the latter, Britain's unique position and special considerations affecting her status in Western defence made it expedient that Britain did not join the EDC immediately. Rather, the intention was that Britain should postpone full participation in the European movement until the supranational functional progress among the Six had mushroomed, as it was expected to, into a fully-fledged Western European political union. This was the Truman-Acheson policy supported by General Eisenhower, who was 'fully in accord ... and worked for it diligently and devotedly from the day of his appointment as Supreme Commander until he returned to the United States in 1952 to enter the political arena'.[18] According to Truman, General Eisenhower advised, in early January 1952, that:

> those countries of the alliance [NATO] on the continent of Europe would have to work toward economic and political consolidation. Britain could not be easily fitted into such a picture, and he agreed with the British that they should be associated with the proposed European Defence Community but not directly take part in it. But there was some hope, in Eisenhower's opinion, that the return of Winston Churchill to the Government in England would mean more emphasis on political union. Eisenhower urged me to persuade Churchill, in his forthcoming visit to Washington, to make 'a ringing statement that would minimize British non-participation and emphasize British moral, political, and military support for the European Army'.[19]

The role of Britain was clearly to be a supportive one from outside. 'I look upon the European Defence force', explained General Eisenhower, 'as a step towards the political and economic union that I believe necessary. Therefore, to my way of thinking, the attempt to include Britain *immediately* would be a stumbling-block rather than a help.'[20] Apart from all else, there was the immediate requirement of a German defence contribution, and though this was uppermost in his mind and he wanted no delay, the General, on occasions, seemed to have no doubt as to the ultimate alternatives facing Britain—'Of course, Britain must decide for herself whether it is in her interest to enter a USE [United States of Europe]. Maybe ultimately your choice is either to become the 49th state or to join the USE.'[21] In the meantime, however, European unity was still facing 'the deadly danger of procrastination, timid measures, slow steps, and cautious stages',[22] which could hardly be alleviated by British participation in negotiations on the proposed European Army. Thus, after the initial inclination to favour British participation, mainly from the standpoint of progress towards political unity, the Truman Administration, supported by General Eisenhower, was quick to welcome Britain's refusal to join the European Army. Acheson himself confirmed this to Eden, saying that 'the Americans had no wish to urge Britain to join EDC'[23] and the Secretary of State and the British Foreign Minister agreed instead on the suitability of a joint declaration, in the form of a new 'Monroe Doctrine' for Europe.[24] At the end of his Presidency, Truman himself could be satisfied with the thought that, while the ratification of the EDC treaty had not met his anticipated schedule,

The structure of Western European Defence had been built – built largely because we were ready to break with tradition and enter into a peace-time military alliance ; because we had been ready to assume not only our share but the leadership in the forging of joint forces ; because we had recognized that the peace of the world would best be served by a Europe that was strong and united, and that, therefore, European unity and European strength were the best guarantees for the prevention of another major war.[25]

But the structure of Western European defence which Truman considered built was one which saw the exclusion of Britain from the proposed EDC with full United States agreement. The role of Britain, as of the United States, was that of supporting the EDC from outside while firmly anchoring the immediate security of the West on the Anglo-American alliance.

From the British rejection of the Schuman Plan, but principally in relation to the creation of a European Defence Community and the organisation of NATO, there had been a radical shift in the Truman policy from its earlier inconsistencies over Britain's role towards an interim acceptance of a 'three-pillar' concept of Atlantic community. This concept was becoming increasingly popular from the time agreement had been reached among the Six at the Paris Conference on the EDC in July 1951. In the following month, a report of the committee of the National Planning Association publicly criticised the Administration's European policy as 'inadequate' and recommended 'political and economic unification of the Continental nations to strengthen Western Europe'.[26] The pamphlet prepared for the National Planning Association's Committee on International Policy[27] by Theodore Geiger and H. Van B. Cleveland, junior members of the State Department, called for a reorganisation of NATO on a tripartite basis:

> The underlying causes of Europe's helplessness can be removed ... by a political union of the Continental countries, within a North Atlantic Treaty Organization reorganized on a tripartite basis.
>   This three-way arrangement would consolidate NATO into component member units—the United States, the United Kingdom and the Commonwealth, and the Continental countries represented as a group through their new supra-national agencies.[28]

The idea that Britain and the Commonwealth should stand on their own as a third pillar or a bridge in the evolving Atlantic community did not stem solely from political-military considerations. Congressman John W. McCormack was among those who found the following views of one commentator in Collier's magazine 'challenging and constructive':

> Nor do the British need union with the continent for the solution of their own problems.... [Britain] already enjoys, in the globe-circling commonwealth and sterling area, membership in a large economic and political unit.... However, there would be marked benefits both for Britain and for the continent if some form of special economic relationship, short of full membership, could be worked out between Britain and the continental union. Similarly, the solution of Britain's persistent balance-of-payments problem may sooner or later require some sort of special economic relationship between Britain and the United States. Thus, Britain might in time become a binding link between the two larger members of the North Atlantic Community, the United States and United Europe.[29]

The salient difference between the Administration's policy and these viewpoints was that the Administration in accepting the realities of the moment, and realising the importance of the Anglo-American alliance and Britain as a bridge to the Continent, did not accept the three-pillar arrangement as a permanent solution but merely as an expedient. In his farewell address to the North Atlantic Council, Secretary Acheson summed up his long-term vision for Atlantic community:

> The European Defence Community, Mr. Acheson declared, has created a centripetal force that, in time, will draw in Britain from across the Channel and the United States and Canada from across the Atlantic in a development whose importance it is 'impossible to overestimate'.[30]

Yet, until the Six fully consolidated themselves in political union, Britain would maintain her special position, and play a special role in the Anglo-American alliance which remained for the Truman Administration the corner-stone of the West.

From the purely military-strategic standpoint of American foreign policy, the EDC was seen as a single unit in the defence of the West, and its task would be the defence of continental Western Europe. German rearmament within EDC, and the efficient organisation of a European Army within NATO were expected, by firmly securing Europe, to facilitate the Truman policy of global containment of Communism in other vital areas. This would be undertaken jointly by the United States and Britain, whose European presence would diminish as the European Army matured. Thus, in November 1951, Eden was informed by General Eisenhower that Britain and the United States 'could be more effective as elements supporting the European Army within the Atlantic Organisation. As the European Army developed, it was thought that maybe we and the Americans could be drawn into reserve. We should be there and available if needed, but it might not be a bad thing if the Europeans could stand on their own'.[31] In Eisenhower's view, EDC was to become a 'hard and dependable core' for NATO,[32] and he fully endorsed Eden's foreign policy statement to the House of Commons of 5 February 1952, which to his mind 'states a correct position for the United Kingdom.'[33] Among the interesting points in that speech, the British Foreign Minister put Britain's relationship to the EDC and NATO in a nutshell:

H

I should like at this point to remind the House of a recent state-ment made by General Eisenhower. After saying that he could see no acceptable alternative to union between the States of Europe, he added that he believed that any attempt to include Britain im-mediately in a European defence force 'would be a stumbling block rather than a help'. In the same speech he asked how the British Commonwealth of Nations could be combined with Western Europe today. It seems to us that the answer to the question is that, as things have now developed, Britain and the Commonwealth could best be linked with Western Europe through the Atlantic Organisa-tion.

That is why it seems to us of capital importance that we should realise that the North Atlantic Treaty is not merely some temporary expedient arising from the threat of Soviet aggression. That is why we regard it as a permanent association, which must be intimate but not exclusive. Our other Commonwealth ties are sacred.[34]

This was as clear a statement as ever in favour of the 'three-pillar' Atlantic community. The significance, however, is in the divergence which it displayed between the Anglo-American regard for the permanence of the Atlantic organisation and Mr Schuman's view that the Atlantic system had to be considered as transient, answering and satisfying 'urgent yet passing needs'. The Anglo-American tendency under Truman and the Conservative Government was distinctly towards a 'three-pillar' Atlantic com-munity, with Britain as a master-link between the United States and Continental Western Europe. But at the same time, the military-strategic organisation of NATO would move towards a functional 'dumb-bell' arrangement on the basis of the Anglo-American alliance, with its global purpose, and the EDC with its European purpose. Another feature that would arise from the formation of EDC within NATO would be the gradual disap-pearance of the multilateral Atlanticist approach in favour of a triangular relationship among the United States, Britain and the Commonwealth, and the EDC with whatever provisions necessary for the non-EDC members of the pact. In practice, however, such a three-way relationship would virtually amount to a straight bilateral Anglo-American and EDC approach. Precisely this type of relationship was already developing in the joint Anglo-American approach to the ratification of EDC. In the communiqué issued at the end of the Washington Conference in January 1952, between President Truman and Prime Minister Churchill, it was declared that:

Our two Governments will continue to give their full support to the efforts now being made to establish a European defence community, and will lend all assistance in their power in bringing it to fruition.... The defence of the free world will be strengthened and solidified by the creation of a European defence community as an element in a constantly developing Atlantic community.[35]

The other main element was the Anglo-American alliance, fully affirmed in the sense of the entire communiqué, which also made it clear that the sanctity of the Commonwealth to which Eden's speech referred was also appreciated by the Truman Administration from the point of view of raw materials. Mr Ernest Davies, formerly Under-Secretary of State for Foreign Affairs with the Labour Government, expressed justifiable concern 'lest there should be any impression from the Anglo-American talks, and the statements which have been made, that we will work out a joint Anglo-American policy which will be presented to the smaller Powers and that pressure will be used upon them to adopt that policy'.[36]

At the end of 1952, with the Democrats on their way out of the Presidential seat, United States policy had fully adjusted itself to an Atlantic community in which Britain and the Commonwealth occupied a middle position between the United States and continental Western Europe, which was expected to unify itself around the nucleus of the Six. The prospects of the supranational movement seemed quite favourable, despite some delay on EDC 'over matters of timing and emphasis, not over principles'.[37] The State Department's inclination towards the Anglo-American alliance had been reconciled with the European movement by the Continental leadership, and by the hard fact of Britain's determined aloofness. The structure of Western European defence had been built, so it seemed to Truman, and European unity seemed within sight. Ultimately, Britain would be drawn from across the Channel but for the short run the Anglo-American alliance had been reaffirmed and strengthened, despite its subjection to tensions in the Far East. The immediate task of Britain was to do its utmost by way of support and encouragement for the success of the EDC.

With the inauguration of President Eisenhower, in January 1953, severe strains began to be placed on the Anglo-American relationship by the Republican Administration, back in office after twenty years. Britain's aloofness from the EDC was reluctantly accepted by the new Secretary of State, John Foster Dulles and on the general issue of Britain's relations with the United States and Western Europe, it was evident from the start that the Republican Administration was prepared to be far less accommodating to British policy than was its predecessor. Apart from the various international frictions between Britain and America, the rot which set into the Anglo-American alliance during the first Eisenhower Administration owed much to the new Republican foreign policy bent, to personality clashes, and to the uncertain attitude of President Eisenhower himself. In the autumn of 1952, General Eisenhower apparently shifted from his view that 'the necessary and wise subordination of the military to civil power will best be sustained when life-long professional soldiers abstain from seeking high political office'.[38] The General had decided to enter the Presidential race. Until he declared his candidature for the Republican Party, which according to Truman had 'appropriated' him, it was generally unknown even in the highest circles where the General stood, as Republican or Democrat.[39] Not only did Eisenhower's faithful service with two Democratic Presidents, and his intimate association with the foreign policy formulation of the outgoing Administration, place him in a rather embarrassing position as the Republican nominee, but the rift within the Republican Party between 'isolationists' and 'internationalists' created a formidable problem in developing a united Republican foreign policy platform.[40]

Whatever views Eisenhower may have had on foreign policy before his election, on becoming President his main concern was to pursue a Republican foreign policy acceptable enough to both extremes of the party. The Truman Administration had come under increasing criticism of appeasement towards Communism, of being pro-British, and of being soft on Western European unity—displaying a 'support it, don't push it' line. In the Korean crisis, Secretary of State Acheson, always suspected in some quarters as being a possible 'fellow traveller', was mercilessly attacked to the point of demands for his immediate dismissal from Republican Asia-Firsters, who accused him of having facilitated a communist victory in China by blocking General MacArthur's strategy.[41] During the Presidential campaign, the Democratic Party fell to 'mass accusations of subversion and corruption'.[42] Eisenhower's acute hypersensitivity to the wave of anti-Democratic criticism made him eager to dissociate himself from Democratic policies and Democrats,[43] and to bend over backwards to please Republican, Congressional, and vocal public opinion quite indiscriminately on practically all issues.

In the conduct of American foreign policy throughout the Eisenhower era, John Foster Dulles was paramount. The choice of Dulles as Secretary of State was for Eisenhower 'an obvious one' — 'Before his appointment he and I had held a number of conversations on the international outlook and found ourselves in substantial agreement in our conclusions. He was a vigorous Republican who had represented bipartisanship in earlier years, a man of strong opinions and unimpeachable character.'[44] For a number of reasons the appointment of Dulles was quite ominous of the downward trend to follow in Anglo-American relations. Both Churchill and Eden had very early expressed great interest in knowing whom Eisenhower would call upon to be Secretary of State if he were to be elected, and Eden went so far as to suggest openly that Eisenhower appoint anyone other than Dulles.[45] Such a suggestion coming from Eden, with whom Eisenhower had had a long association and was used to the frankest exchanges, was 'understandable'; from anyone else, however, he would have resented it as 'an unwarranted intrusion in America's affairs'.[46] This seemed to set the tone of Anglo-American relations under Eisenhower. It might not have been so, but for the completely free rein which Eisenhower allowed Dulles over foreign policy.

... Dulles, not Eisenhower, was the prime mover of American foreign policy. It was he who generated it. It was he who persuaded the President. It was he who carried it forward. It made Dulles the effective commander of American power for the six years of his Secretaryship. And the world recognized him as such.[47]

Republican foreign policy was principally a combination of 'Asia-First' and 'Fortress America' ideas — the one manifest in the preoccupation of preventing the spread of Communism in Asia; the other symbolised in the Dullesian strategic doctrine of massive retaliation. Dulles, though never underestimating the importance of Western Europe, held the view that Stalin had laid down an 'Asia-First' strategy for the Soviet Union in 1924, which was still being followed.[48]

The consequences for Western Europe of the primacy which Dulles personally attached to Asia and the Pacific area were profound, and to the British even amounted to perfidy within the Anglo-American relationship. A major interest was still main-

tained under the Republicans in Western Europe, but this was
largely a matter of trying to bulldoze the continental countries
into acceptance of the European Army and into European unity,
thereby consolidating the region so that the United States could
give most of its attention to Asia.

The sinews of Republican policy towards Western Europe and
the Atlantic Community were immediately evidenced in the tour
of the various European capitals, in January 1953, by Secretary
Dulles and Harold Stassen, Director of the Mutual Security
Agency, for the purpose of pushing the ratification of EDC,[49]
and by the new American approach at the NATO Council Paris
Conference, in April. It was apparent even in these first four
months that the Eisenhower Administration was making radical
departures from its predecessor's policy. The reasonable optimistic
outlook on EDC[50] by the Truman Administration at the end of
1952 — disagreement but 'not over principles' — was thrust aside
in a dramatic haste to stampede the Six into ratifying the EDC
treaty, leaving no chance for it to wither on the vine. The
Republican pressure for EDC was underlined by a switch in the
emphasis of United States foreign policy under Dulles to the Far
East, and by a change in strategic orientation from the building
up of large ground forces, which was the Truman policy, to reliance on nuclear weapons, and air and naval power, which seemed
to fit the natural role of the United States. These changes were
apparent beneath the decisions arrived at in the Paris NATO
conference. But the Republican 'New Look' policy advocated at
the NATO conference also stemmed from very basic domestic
considerations. It was a feature of the Eisenhower Administration
to demonstrate unusual deference to Congressional opinion on
practically all matters,[51] and particularly in anxiously trying to
redeem its platform pledges of cutting back on military and
other forms of appropriations.[52] Congress itself, given the situation in Korea and the Far East generally, was increasingly
giving ground to its 'Asia-Firster', 'Fortress-America', and isolationist elements. As far as Western Europe was concerned, there
was unrelenting clamour for immediate ratification of EDC and
the unification of Western Europe as a condition of further
American aid — the so-called 'or else' policy.[53] Certainly, Congress was in no extravagant mood, especially towards Western
Europe. In desperately trying to gain early political victories in

the eyes of Congress, the Eisenhower Administration gradually lost much of its initiative in foreign policy to Congress.

One effect of the Congressional vigilance over foreign policy was the Eisenhower Administration's slash of $1·8 billion off the Truman foreign aid programme and the introduction of the 'stretch-out' and 'long-haul' concepts announced at the NATO conference in Paris. Significantly enough, however, the Administration's real cut was in appropriations to Western Europe, while aid to the Far East was substantially increased, without preventing the net reduction in the budget required to meet election promises. The switch in foreign assistance from Western Europe to Asia went hand in hand with the Dulles view at Paris that the Western European countries and not the United States should be the pacemakers in NATO:

... we all agree that the NATO organization and its programme must proceed. There is considerable reason to believe that the European members of the Council should, in a sense, be the pacemakers. They are here and appreciate the peril perhaps better than we do ; but the United States is fully prepared to continue to take the major role in developing here the force in being which is needed to deter aggression.[54]

But in endeavouring 'to obtain the maximum military strength with the minimum of money' for NATO,[55] and in suggesting that the Europeans be the 'pacemakers' in NATO, Dulles could hardly escape giving the impression that, as far as he was concerned, NATO was primarily a European baby and that it was up to the Europeans to set the pace in strengthening the organisation by ratifying EDC. Indeed, the threat of an 'agonising reappraisal' of American policy which later underpinned pressures for the ratification of the EDC was already evident at this stage in Dulles' attitude towards NATO and his basic 'Asia-First' outlook. The reappraisal was already being implemented in the Administration's determination to shift the burdens of Western European defence substantially on to the Europeans themselves and on to the EDC, in an effort not merely to satisfy Congressional clamour for European unity but to permit increased American attention and assistance to Far Eastern defence. As a significant step in the Administration's policy, there was the repudiation of the 1952 Lisbon goals at the Paris conference for 'stretchout' and 'long-haul' calculations affecting NATO. These saw a decrease in the 1953 and 1954 targets for planes from 6,500 to 5,500 (for 1953) and from 9,000 to 7,000 (for 1954), with a corresponding reduction in targets for divisions from 75 to 60, and from 96 to 70. Commenting on the American decisions at Paris, the Alsop brothers wryly observed that:

As it is perhaps carping to recall, NATO Supreme Commander Eisenhower initially asked no less than 120 divisions for Western Europe. This figure was cut over the general's protest, to the 100 divisions agreed at the Lisbon meeting. When the President was a general, this figure was a minimum; now, however, NATO is to have 56 divisions by the end of this year, and indefinite additional strength in a highly indefinite future.[56]

The change in defence targets, ostensibly to provide for quality not quantity, as well as for maximum economy to meet a 'permanent' emergency rather than a more or less fixed-dated threat, which was the basis of the military planning of the Truman Administration, facilitated the switch to an 'Asia-First' policy while it drove home to the Europeans just how much their own defence would in future depend on their own efforts. Similarly, the doctrine of massive retaliation provided a strategic rationalisation for the Eisenhower Administration's 'Asia-First' policy. This presented the Western Europeans with a painful American guarantee based largely on the credibility of the United States nuclear threat in defence of Europe, which most Europeans found quite incredible.

The irony of the Eisenhower Administration's defence policies, with the switch in emphasis to Asia, was that it was largely predicated upon the ratification of EDC under American pressure. Dulles' interest in Western Europe may be summed up as seeing the completion of the process of reconstituting the Federal Republic, and rearming the Germans within EDC, while seeing EDC as the mainstay of Western European security and the final step towards Western European unity. It has been said of the Secretary of State that in Asia his nose followed Chiang Kai-shek, while in Europe his ear was set on Adenauer. In fact, there is precious little ground for disagreement with this comment. Dulles had little attachment to ideas of Atlantic community, and largely perceived a strong united Western Europe, for which he had always been one of the staunchest advocates, as essentially a satellite of the United States of America and a condition precedent for the all-out American pursuit of liberation and roll-back policies against communism in Asia.

Although the Republican Administration had to accept the fact of British non-participation in the EDC, its attitudes and policies towards Britain's role in relation to Western Europe nevertheless differed fundamentally from those of the Truman Administration. In this connection, the attitude of President Eisenhower, which was essentially nearer to that of the Truman Administration, was in practice dominated by the attitude of Secretary of State Dulles. Moreover, even though Eisenhower maintained something of a special position for Britain, the deep-seated frictions between United States and British policy over Korea, Indo-China, the People's Republic of China, and the Middle East, together with the attitudes of Secretary of State Dulles and of Congress, had a rather chilling effect on the President's attitude towards Britain. The result was his conspicuous efforts to play down the Anglo-American relationship, and to treat Britain more or less as just another ally.

If, on becoming President, Eisenhower tended to underplay the Anglo-American alliance, his Secretary of State virtually refused to recognise it at all. It could be expected that Dulles' primary attachment to the Far East and Britain's secondary interests there would constitute a weak link in the Anglo-American alliance. Another weakening influence was Dulles' increasing reliance on the United States nuclear strike, which tended to diminish the earlier importance of the Anglo-American alliance, while in general encouraging the attitude that alliances had shifted from being basic guarantees of United States military security to buffers against the spread of international Communism in the most vulnerable areas. In practice, the development of the American nuclear deterrent also encouraged the view that countries in alliance with the United States were in all respects dependent on America, and that consequently their policies should be kept in line with Washington. In the distribution of power within the West, equality and interdependence between the United States and her various allies were now hardly more than a mere diplomatic pretence. Reality was otherwise. Particularly with the pontifical anti-Communist exhortations with which Dulles imbued American foreign policy,[57] this type of attitude was a constant source of annoyance to Britain, which had looked to her influence on Washington as an important aspect of her postwar international status. Eden in a message to the British Ambassador to Washington, for instruction to Dulles, painfully made the point that:

Americans may think the time past when they need consider the feelings or difficulties of their allies. It is the conviction that this tendency becomes more pronounced every week and is creating mounting difficulties for anyone in this country who wants to maintain close Anglo-American relations.[58]

Eden, of course, never fancied Dulles from the start and came to regard him as 'a preacher in a world of politics'.[59] Indeed, much of the difficulties in Anglo-American relationships related to the personal frictions between Eden and Dulles, and it is evident that Eden's relations with the Secretary of State were neither very cordial nor intimate.[60] On the other hand, Dulles' very close relationships with Monnet and Adenauer contrasted with his weak personal ties in the top echelons of British politics, and pointed to his preference for a Continental link rather than an Anglo-American 'special relationship'.[61] Nothing in fact was more irritating to Dulles than the British claim to a 'special relationship' with the United States,[62] and apart from sharing all the worst American prejudices against British imperialism, Dulles had no understanding of and little concern for the Commonwealth,[63] which he regarded as a vague instrument for maintaining Britain's illusions of power.

On the issue of Britain's role in relation to Western Europe, Dulles' attitude was quite basic—Britain's position ought to be in a united Europe. Dulles was in full accord with the ardent 'Europeanists' in Congress and would have found little disagreement with Senator Fulbright's view that:

... a European union without Britain would lack realism and for that reason British membership would be a prime requisite. It seems to me that there are no insurmountable obstacles in the way of Britain fulfilling her obligations in both federations [i.e. the Commonwealth and a united Western Europe] with injury neither to herself nor to any other state. Indeed there is reason to believe that by her possession of membership in both, Britain would play a larger role in the quest for world peace.[64]

Dulles, however, did not see the Commonwealth as any kind of unity, federal or otherwise, and by the time he became Secretary of State he had a long-standing annoyance with Britain over her refusal to move either here or there in regard to Commonwealth or Western European unity. Early in the day, in January 1948, Dulles had pointed out that:

any Customs union between the Marshall Plan countries would be greatly strengthened by the inclusion of Britain. 'If you develop unity within the British Commonwealth', he said, 'it would be a magnificent thing. It would also be a magnificent thing to develop unity with Europe, but to stand in a state of indecision is not a magnificent thing.'[65]

Thus there is some substance in Goold-Adams' estimation that what Dulles blamed the British for in general was 'that they failed to make the most of themselves'.[66] By 1953 it appeared to Dulles that Britain had managed to overcome her state of indecision by simply deciding to do nothing, which in his reasoning had the effect, if not the intention, of impeding continental efforts towards unity. The problem of European unity, as M. Spaak so rightly pointed out at Strasbourg, was 'willy-nilly dominated by that of the participation of Great Britain in the European effort, and by Great Britain's attitude to this problem'.[67] Dulles was sympathetic to the Benelux fears of a Continental union dominated by a Franco-German axis; he understood French anxieties about a Continental union dominated by Germany; he was partial to Germany and saw the full integration of the Federal Republic within a united Western Europe as the major goal of America's European policy: but he simply could not understand why Britain, the principal solution to these problems, could not join the European movement, and why Britain, already a third-class power and doomed to Castilian decadence if she did not join a united Western Europe, should exert her influence towards disunity rather than unity on the Continent. For Dulles' appraisal of Britain's diplomacy was tinged with the subtle logic that not being for unity she was against it, not only for herself but for all Western Europe —and he could look at the British posture on economic integration, on the Council of Europe, on the Schuman Plan, on the EDC: he could see the alignment of the Scandinavian countries behind Britain, and point to the consistent British reluctance to give the Six the leadership and reassurance for which they asked.

On the issue of the EDC Dulles, like Truman, Acheson and Eisenhower, had to accept the fact of British non-participation. But by both his words and his actions he leaves no doubt that his acceptance of the reality was shrouded in his conviction that Britain had no real alternative role apart from joining Europe and that the chances of the EDC succeeding without Britain were minimal. Dulles, probably more than anyone else in America, was quite pessimistic about the EDC's chances:

So far as Europe is concerned [he wrote] it must, I think, be taken as doubtful that there will be time to create an effective European army at the rate this is now moving, or perhaps even at the optimum rate.[68]

Although this was written before the European Army proposal really got off the ground, the pressures which Dulles later placed for the ratification of the EDC treaty stemmed as much from considerations of time in finding a solution to German rearmament, as from fear that ratification if it were to come at all could only come under tremendous American pressures, and maximum British support to the Six. While looking for far-reaching British support to the EDC, his attitude towards Britain was strongly influenced by his personal conviction that Britain should really be in the EDC. Even before the EDC had been proposed, Dulles had made the following comment on the problem besetting Western European defence:

In the problem of military defense, while progress has been made, it is not along the lines which hold any assurance of success. No one of the countries of Western Europe is able to develop a military establishment which would be formidable on its own account ... the English want a defense of their own, the French want a defense of their own, Benelux wants a defense of its own, and so forth. It is not possible with the resources available, to build a formidable and effective defense out of a series of politically distinct military establishments.[69]

Within a week of becoming Secretary of State, Dulles gave the menacing warning that:

If France, Germany and England should go their separate ways, then certainly it would be necessary to give a little rethinking to America's own foreign policy in relation to Western Europe.[70]

Ironically, it was France which all along proved the main stumbling block to EDC and which finally brought it down.[71] On 19 March 1953, the Federal Republic ratified the EDC treaty. There followed the ratifications by the Netherlands, Belgium and Luxembourg, leaving, by the spring of 1954, only France and Italy to give final parliamentary approval to the treaty. Opposition to the EDC was, however, on the upswing in both countries. Growing last-minute doubts found nourishment in the Russian 'peace offensive' which followed the death of Stalin a year earlier, on 5 March 1953, and the ending of the Korean War. Italy was undergoing a period of political instability and seemed content to bring up the rear on EDC by awaiting French action. In France the Laniel Government fell on 12 June over the Indo-China issue, and six days later M. Mendès-France assumed the Premiership. He immediately demonstrated his own personal doubts about the prospects of French ratification by proposing amendments to the EDC treaty, in an effort to make it more palatable to the Assembly, but he lacked the necessary support from the other signatories. The EDC treaty was finally presented for debate in the French Assembly on 28 August. Debate was brief. On 30 August the treaty was summarily rejected by France on a count of 319 votes to 264 with 43 abstentions.

In the critical and agonising stages of the EDC fiasco, between January 1953 and August 1954, Britain was allocated a very important role by the United States as prime mover in facilitating the ratification of EDC. Whereas under the Truman Administration there were joint Anglo-American efforts to encourage the ratification of EDC, Anglo-American declarations of support, reassurances, and guarantees to the French and the other members of the proposed community, as well as to the community itself; under the Eisenhower Administration there was a distinct absence of the spirit of cooperation between the two countries which had characterised their earlier approach to the EDC. Admittedly, this was partly due to the strained personal relationship between Dulles and Eden. But the significant reason was that under the Eisenhower Administration Britain's role became in effect that of a necessary junior functionary in getting the Continentals, particularly the French, to ratify EDC. Britain's position as a bridge between the United States and continental Western Europe was disrobed of any real semblance of a 'special relationship'. Instead, her influence on the Continent was the dominating factor, and the American relationship with Britain was one of simple convenience in which Britain was expected to exercise her influence in Western Europe according to the policies laid down in Washington. The Dullesian concept of Atlantic community was entirely 'two-pillar' — North America and Western Europe. Instead of adjusting to the temporary expedient of a 'three-pillar' framework, with Britain and the Commonwealth as a link-pin between the United States and Continental Western Europe, Dulles determinedly concentrated on the idea of a completely united Western Europe to be built around the nucleus of the Six, and saw Britain simply as the

important odd man out without recognisable or justifiable claim
to a special position. Britain was for all practical purposes treated
as essentially a European power. Her thesis that, given her
Commonwealth ties, her world-wide role, her junior membership
of the nuclear club, she was not only different from the Continental countries but was under no obligation to associate herself
any closer with the Continental countries than was the United
States, had little meaning to Dulles, other than signifying Britain's
illusions about her future role and rationalising her intentions of
continuing her traditional European balance of power diplomacy.
Dulles' attitude was that Britain was an integral part of Western
Europe, and he was quite annoyed by Britain's refusal to accept
her station, and by her persistent pretensions about Commonwealth
unity and 'special relationship'. He was convinced that, had
Britain joined the supranational movement in the Schuman Plan
and the EDC, there would be no problems in the way of the
latter. Consequently, while reluctantly accepting that nothing
could be done to persuade Britain to join the EDC, Dulles saw it
as Britain's obligation to ensure the ratification of EDC by all
possible means. The United States would certainly make every
effort in this direction, but it was principally up to Britain to bring
the proposal into being. Such responsibility lay as much with
Britain, even though she was not party to the treaty, as with the
Six, and the consequences of the failure to realise EDC—the
threatened 'agonising reappraisal'—would carry its disadvantages
for Britain and the Continent without discrimination. 'Always we
moved in concert with the British', declares Eisenhower in his
memoirs,[72] but this picture of concerted Anglo-American efforts
can be misleading. The working relationship between the United
States and Britain to bring about the ratification of EDC was an
uneasy and fragile one, based neither on any equality in the degree
of interest nor extensive similarity in motive behind the end
sought. From the British side, it was reluctant, pessimistic, and
forged out of sheer expediency in trying against all odds to secure
the Anglo-American alliance and to obviate any possibility of
the threatened 'reappraisal' which Eden did not at all take as a
bluff.[73] Above all, the relationship was patently one in which the
United States dictated the end to be achieved and, apart from
some occasional diplomatic interventions on a background of
constant menacing of the Europeans, left it mainly to Britain to
find whatever means there were of allaying continental misgivings.

In short, it was a concert in which Secretary of State Dulles assumed the role of indefatigable conductor, and with a large baton summoned Britain to fiddle so that Europe could sing in unison once more. According to the British Foreign Secretary:

... I had an important conversation with Mr Dulles. What he told me on this occasion was much in my mind throughout the following year, and particularly after the failure of EDC. On the evening he came to see me, Mr Dulles had spoken at a press conference of the 'agonising reappraisal' of American policy, which would have to take place if France failed to ratify EDC. ... The United States Government felt that it was essential to give French public opinion a jolt. The French, he said, did not seem to be aware of the very grave consequences upon American policy if the hopes of a European arrangement, which would unite France and Germany, were to be dashed. He had been speaking to M. Jean Monnet and had reached the conclusion that it was probably not possible to find a French Government which could put through EDC and govern France, since the majorities required for these two purposes were different. ... *Mr Dulles continued that it might be necessary to work for a French Government which could take office solely for the purpose of putting through EDC. ...*

Mr Dulles then told me that he thought we, by which he apparently meant the United States and Britain, were approaching a parting of the ways with regard to American policy. If things went wrong, the United States might swing over to a policy of western hemispheric defence, with the emphasis on the Far East. ... *Mr Dulles pointed out that the consequences of a swing of American policy towards hemispheric defence were of obvious concern to Great Britain. He hoped, therefore, that I might find occasion to underline the warnings which he had issued in his statement, and make some appeal to France.*[74]

The statement is a fair testimony to the changed nature of the Anglo-American relationship. Acheson had on occasion found it necessary to remind the British that the power of the West had been transferred to the United States, and that Britain ought to stop deceiving herself about her ability to maintain her traditional world role indefinitely, as the changed circumstances of the post-war world left her with no long-term future outside a united Western Europe, where her leadership was necessary. Nevertheless, Acheson's foreign policies demonstrated an understanding of the British imperial dilemma, and despite its contradictions, tended to give Britain a 'special' position in a close Anglo-American partnership built as much out of necessity as out of sympathetic recognition of the many bonds between the two countries. Dulles gave Britain no 'special' position in American policy, never forgot to underline that Britain was the weaker power, and in his desperate pursuit of the vanishing shadow of EDC Britain was indeed the 'whipping boy'.[75]

7

Western European Union and the parting of the ways

There was prompt reaction to the collapse of the EDC on both sides of the Atlantic. The Eisenhower Administration made clear its intention of immediately bringing Germany directly into NATO even in face of French opposition. At the same time the American Chiefs of Staff began their strategic reappraisal in the light of the failure to place European defence on an effective united European footing. On the other side of the Atlantic, it was the British Government which was demonstrating the greatest anxiety about the probable consequences of the collapse of EDC, and which was making the greatest effort to salvage the situation as best it could. In this connection Eden was quick in evolving a plan which he hoped would rescue the main elements of the American interest in EDC. It was clear that the Americans had left it up to the British to perform the rescue operation, and on 14 September, only two weeks after the French rejection of EDC, Dulles set off for London to have discussions with Eden on the line of action which the British Foreign Secretary was developing. On his departure Dulles left a note stating:

I am going to London at the invitation of the British Government to consider plans for *European Defence. Heretofore, European defence planning has taken place under the North Atlantic Treaty* [and] it has been assumed that Germany would be assured the EDC. Now it is necessary to seek an alternative.[1]

Dulles' departure for London came in the middle of a hectic tour of European capitals by Eden, between 11–17 September, in which Eden was trying to sell his two point salvage plan as it then stood:

(a) German entry into NATO with safeguards over German re-armament of a non-discriminatory character, and the con-

I

centration of all military arrangements within the NATO framework;

(b)   The expansion of the Brussels Treaty for use as a political instrument to keep alive the idea of European unity.[2]

In his message to Eden informing him of his decision to visit Bonn and London, Dulles had made it clearly understood that 'he was critical of the plan for expanding the Brussels Treaty, and he would regard any solution which did not provide for the creation of a supranational institution as "makeshift" '.[3] Both President Eisenhower and Dulles had been kept informed of Eden's progress with the Continental leaders through Churchill, and on the day on which Dulles set off for Bonn and London Eden had notified the American Secretary of State of the warm welcome which the British proposals had received in Germany and in the Benelux countries.[4] Dulles' critical attitude to the Eden plan and his sudden intervention at this point in Eden's tour, which Eden received as a shock,[5] are, therefore, of major significance in understanding subsequent developments, particularly the ultimate historic commitment of British troops to the continent. In fact, Dulles' real purpose in coming to London was to ensure that whatever arrangements were being made by Eden, they would in their final outcome approximate as closely as possible to the military unity of Western Europe envisaged in the EDC, with prospects for major progress to political unity. What he certainly did not intend to have was the far-reaching aspirations of the EDC replaced by yet another watered-down British alternative to full-fledged European integration.

Dulles was in every sense an ardent supporter of Western European unity, and an appreciation of this is essential to a proper understanding of his attitude towards the EDC and his grave disappointment over the failure of the proposal. The roots of his support for the EDC proposal may be traced to his original misgivings over the nature of the American commitment to Western Europe in the form of the Atlantic Pact, and to his approach to the German problem. In the bipartisan discussions on the nature of an American commitment during the spring of 1948, Dulles had expressed his fear that 'any firm commitment, either military or economic, would be used by the Governments of Western Europe as an excuse to continue their own social and economic experiments'.[6] He had also argued consistently that 'any permanent arrangement [i.e. commitment] might seem to guarantee the *status quo* and make it less likely, rather than more likely, that the Western European democracies would unite to create greater strength between themselves'.[7] On the German problem, Dulles had from that time seen the solution as requiring 'first of all [the] rapid strengthening and unification of our Western allies. So long as there is weakness and disunity of the Brussels Pact Powers, that requires them to seek the weakness and disunity of Germany'.[8] Dulles had fully recognised the value of the creation of the BTO as a step towards European unity. But his own conception of the future relationship which the United States should have with the BTO departed from that of the Truman Administration in his conviction that 'the Atlantic Pact should be looked upon primarily as adding the power of the United States and Canada to the Brussels Pact Powers so that the Germans may be permitted unity'.[9] This was essentially a two-pillar, or what has since come to be called a 'dumb-bell' approach, and in effect this is precisely what he had hoped the EDC would finally achieve. With the failure of the EDC, Dulles now wanted an alternative which would go as far as possible towards bringing this about, and the entire EDC struggle had served to convince him of the essential relationship between successfully achieving any such solution and the need for direct British involvement in Western Europe and particularly in Western European defence.

In the meeting between Dulles and Eden on 17 September, Eden reported that in all the capitals except France, where discussions had been more difficult, he had received 'a hundred per cent agreement' with his proposals as they stood, and he wondered whether Dulles thought a nine-power conference could therefore be profitably held, and if there was anything further that could be done to prepare for it.[10] Dulles' reaction could not have been very encouraging. He had already expressed in advance his basic criticism of the Eden proposals, in that any solution which did not provide for a supranational institution would be regarded as nothing more than 'makeshift'. There can be no doubt that at this meeting Dulles must have brought considerable pressure on Eden to inject some kind of supranational element into his proposals in order to render them acceptable to the United States. He certainly lost no time in reminding Eden that the American Chiefs of Staff were still occupied with their strategic reappraisal, and had not yet reached their conclusions.[11] According to Eden, Dulles felt that 'it was really immaterial whether a NATO plus Brussels solution was better or worse than EDC. Congress has been "sold" on the latter as the means of uniting Europe, which would then be capable of standing on its own feet without American help.'[12] Eden further states that Dulles added that the future for foreign aid was 'highly doubtful' and that the British 'must assume that continued American participation in Europe, on the present scale and in the present form, was impossible.'[13] Moreover, Dulles emphasised that President Eisenhower's declaration of commitment to the EDC had had the greatest difficulty in receiving Congressional support, and that Britain 'should not rely upon them being repeated for the plan now under consideration'.[14] In subsequent conversations with Churchill, Dulles made precisely the same points, before agreeing to attend the scheduled nine-power conference in London.[15]

On Dulles' departure from London, the British immediately began re-studying their defence planning.[16] It was at this stage that Eden concluded that in carrying his proposals to the London Conference it might be 'wise to have something in reserve' and that 'this could best take the form of a practical move on our part, to show our friends in Europe that we were in earnest'.[17] Thus, after the Dulles-Eden talks, Eden is seen dramatically shifting his ground from viewing the expansion of the Brussels Treaty merely 'for use as a political instrument to keep alive the idea of European unity'[18] to that of trying, in addition, to ensure within the expanded BTO the closest approximation to the unity in European defence which the EDC had offered. Rather than being secondary to the direct inclusion of Germany in NATO, the value of the BTO as a framework for consolidating European defence had now become the primary consideration. To achieve this particular end, maximum French cooperation was necessary, which in turn meant maximum British commitment well beyond the extent that Britain had been prepared to go in relation to EDC. Bevin's thesis had been turned on its heels: instead of the British going no further into Europe than the United States would go, Eden was convinced that if the United States were to remain in Europe at all, then the British would have to go far further into Europe than the United States would ever go, and than the British ever contemplated going. In his memorandum to Churchill informing the Prime Minister of his decision in favour of a far-reaching British commitment, Eden explained his position accordingly:

I realise that this would be an unprecedented commitment for the United Kingdom, but the hard fact is that it is impossible to organise an effective defence system in Western Europe, which in turn is essential for the security of the United Kingdom, without a major British contribution. This situation will persist for many years to come. By recognising this fact and giving the new commitment, we may succeed in bringing the Germans and the French together, and keeping the Americans in Europe.[19]

To this end the fundamental element in the success of the London Conference from 28 September—3 October, 1954 was the historic British pledge that:

Her Majesty the Queen of the United Kingdom of Great Britain and Northern Ireland will continue to maintain on the mainland of Europe including Germany, the effective strength of the United Kingdom forces which are now assigned to the Supreme Allied Commander Europe, that is to say four divisions and the Second Tactical Air Force, or such other forces as the Supreme Allied Commander Europe regards as having equivalent fighting capacity. She undertakes not to withdraw these forces against the wishes of the majority of the High Contracting Parties who should take their decision in the knowledge of the views of the Supreme Allied Commander Europe. This undertaking shall not, however, bind her in the event of an acute overseas emergency. If the maintenance of the United Kingdom forces on the mainland of Europe throws at any time too great a strain on the external finances of the United Kingdom, she will, through Her Government in the United Kingdom of Great Britain and Northern Ireland, invite the North Atlantic Council to review the financial conditions on which the United Kingdom formations are maintained.

This commitment was embodied as Article 6 of Protocol No. 11 (On Forces On Western European Union) in the Final Act of the London Conference and cleared the way for the successful negotiations of the Paris Agreement of 23 October 1954. The Paris Agreements emerged from the London Conference (28 September–3 October 1954),[20] the Paris Conference (20–22 October 1954)[21] and a Ministerial Meeting of the NATO Council (23 October 1954).[22] In substance they covered three broad subjects—Germany, the creation of Western European Union, and the Franco-German dispute over the Saar. It was agreed to terminate the Allied High Commission and Occupation Statute in Germany, and that the Federal Republic should be granted full sovereignty[23] simultaneously with its accession to NATO and its participation in Western European Union. German force levels were to be limited to those previously agreed under EDC, twelve divisions, unless increased levels were given prior unanimous approval by the members of Western European Union. This was a general stipulation applying as well to all participants in Western European Union, with the exception that the maximum of forces of Britain and Luxembourg were not defined according to the EDC requirement.[24] All forces, with the exception of those intended for the defence of overseas territories and those recognised by NATO as suitable to remain under national control, were to be placed under the authority of the Supreme Allied Commander Europe, whose responsibilities and authority were extended to facilitate the integration of such forces.

Western European Union itself was created by agreement to extend the Brussels Treaty Organisation to include the Federal Republic of Germany and Italy, and to rename the expanded organisation accordingly. Under WEU the original structure of the Brussels Treaty was reinforced, particularly with the replacement of the Consultative Council by the Council of WEU which was provided with powers of decision. At the same time, it was decided to extend the activities of WEU beyond the terms of the BTO. One important aspect of this was the determination of the maximum defence contribution to NATO by special agreement and unanimous consent of the members of WEU. Equally important was the agreement to establish an Agency for the control of armaments on the Continent with respect to the development of certain categories of weapons by the continental members of WEU. If the Agency were to find that its prohibitions were being ignored, then it would report to the Council which would decide the issue on the basis of a majority vote.[25] Finally, there was the settlement of the outstanding issue of the Saar by separate Franco-German agreement on a new statute within the framework of WEU.[26]

Proper evaluation of the Paris Agreements cannot be undertaken solely in relation to the hopes originally held out by EDC. An additionally significant consideration would necessarily be the prospects and alternatives existing after the collapse of EDC. In this dual context, the body of agreements signed at Paris probably represented the highest point of attainable compromise on the dramatic curve struck by the EDC episode. The agreements can hardly be regarded as a major victory for anyone, except perhaps Germany. At the same time, however, in terms of

American interest in Western European unity they amounted to the least which the United States was prepared to accept for overlooking its 'agonising reappraisal', and to more than Britain was initially prepared to offer. Even so, the limitation on the exercise of British sovereignty contained in Britain's commitment carried with it such reservation as to afford no serious embarrassment, while the commitment was also presented in the form of a voluntary concession—'a practical move on our part, to show our friends in Europe that we were in earnest.'[27] In a sense, too, WEU could be viewed as the culmination of Britain's postwar European policy as originally laid down by Bevin,[28] and the Conservatives were also able to see it as fulfilling their continuing interest in paramountcy within Western Union while maintaining the Commonwealth link and trying to foster the Anglo-American relationship. From the standpoint of the European movement, the Paris Agreements could be interpreted as being little more than a command to 'as you were'. Yet even on the first account, the Paris Agreements were an important and swift stabiliser for a movement, the back of which had near been broken on the rack of EDC.

Official reaction in the United States to the Paris Agreements was very favourable and enthusiastic. Dulles had opened the London Conference pointing out that

the history of United States action toward Europe – both our positive and our negative action – showed that we responded in many ways like a barometer to the climate which existed in Europe. 'If,' I said, 'the climate is one of unity and cohesion, our assistance and aid of every kind goes out. If the climate is one of dissension, disunity and revival of threats of war . . . then our tendency is to withdraw.'[29]

At the present time 'a great wave of disillusionment had swept over the United States'[30] but, nevertheless, he informed the Conference that he would certainly be willing to recommend that the President renew his pledge to Western Europe:

If, out of the elements of the situation with which we are dealing, if by using the Brussels treaty as a nucleus, it is possible to find in this new pattern a continuing hope of unity among the countries of Europe that are represented here, and if the hopes that were tied in the European Defence Community treaty can reasonably be transferred into the arrangements which will be the outgrowth of this meeting. . . .[31]

After Eden's announcement of the British commitment, Dulles noted that 'from that moment on, all of us meeting in London felt that our efforts were bound to succeed.... The rewards of success had mounted to unexpected heights, and the price of failure had become prohibitive.'[32]

At the end of the London Conference, Dulles informed President Eisenhower of its results, saying:

> I believe that if what is done here is finally realized, we will have saved most of the values inherent in EDC. The Brussels Council will have many supranational responsibilities, and while the present arrangements do not go as far as EDC in creating parliamentary controls, this disadvantage is to an extent offset by the British commital to continental Europe....[33]

Not only the Secretary of State, but the President and the entire Administration were 'highly gratified by developments'.[34] It was Eisenhower's belief that Western European Union 'will promote progress toward unity in Western Europe' and 'will provide a core of unity at the heart of the North Atlantic Treaty Organization'.[35] Accordingly, in March 1955 the United States renewed the pledge which it had originally given to the EDC, to Western European Union. It promised to maintain such armed forces in Europe 'as may be necessary and appropriate ... while a threat to that area exists'.[36] From the standpoint of Germany, the President and his Secretary of State agreed that the Paris Agreements completed a transformation which was a 'near miracle—a shining chapter in history'.[37] In terms of the European movement, Dulles expected that 'Western European unity would be developed through a Council of Western European Union ... the members to consist of the six Continental countries which would have formed the European Defence Community, plus the United Kingdom'.[38] On the very important issue of European defence organisation Dulles was quite satisfied. He maintained that:

> ... through the controls to be exercized through the Council of Western European Union and through the enlarged powers of the Supreme Commander [i.e. to integrate the forces and facilities assigned to him], there will in fact be approximated the military unity which was sought under the European Defence Community Treaty.[39]

On this occasion, Dulles felt there was little ground for pessimism about ratification of the Agreements, particularly as 'the balance in favour of positive action has been weighted by elements which were heretofore lacking, most conspicuously the new commitment of the United Kingdom'.[40] Dulles especially emphasised that:

> ...essentially the present plan for European unity is a plan made by the Europeans for the Europeans. Nothing less would have sufficed. What needed to be proved, and what I think has been proved, is that the Western European people themselves still possess the capacity to respond with resourcefulness to the great challenge of our times.[41]

The essential ingredient in making such a response possible was, of course, the historic British commitment:

> *This declaration marked a basic change in British foreign policy. Heretofore for a century and more, Britain has avoided fixed Continental commitments in favour of its Commonwealth policy. Now, Britain, recognizing that modern developments have largely obliterated the Channel, was ready to identify itself irrevocably with Continental Europe.*[42]

That was the Administration's hope after the creation of WEU. But WEU did not mean for Britain any change in her attitude towards European unity, and was intended only to bolster the Anglo-American alliance while avoiding an 'agonising reappraisal' of American policy towards Western Europe. It was in the next phase of the European movement of the Six that Washington awoke to this fact. By New Year 1956, after the British withdrawal in November 1955 from the preliminary negotiations on the European Common Market and Euratom, the United States and Britain reached a complete parting of the ways with respect to Western Europe. American suspicions of British motives returned as a profound fear of British sabotage of the European movement. It seemed that Britain had purposely withheld the commitment which it gave to WEU from the EDC simply to undermine the supranational scheme. This, at any rate, was the conviction of Dulles which gradually took root in American policy from the middle fifties. On the turbulent background of Anglo-American relations over the Suez crisis, which clearly belied any notion of 'special relationship', it eventually contributed to a virtually complete rupture between the two countries on the issue of Western European unity, lasting until the historic British 'change of heart' in the Kennedy–Macmillan era.

Epilogue

Throughout this period, 1947 to 1956, there had been fundamental divergences between the United States and Britain over Britain's role in the postwar evolution of a new Western Europe. On the one hand, the policy of Western system building and containment introduced by the Truman Doctrine committed the United States to the long-term goal of Western European unity, and this meant not only active support for the European movement but pressures under the ERP and in the case of the EDC for the economic and military integration of Western Europe. The United States instinctively looked to Britain for leadership of the European movement, and tended to expect Britain to see her own salvation in the postwar world as lying in such a course. On the other hand, successive British Governments persistently resisted attempts to fit Britain into a primarily European role during the postwar era and sought instead to maintain Britain's traditional world role. If Ernest Bevin had visions of Britain occupying the central position in a Western Union supported militarily by an Atlantic alliance, and economically by 'the closest possible collaboration with the Commonwealth and with overseas territories, not only British but French, Dutch, Belgian and Portuguese',[1] the Conservative Government which followed the Labour Governments of 1945 to 1951 differed only in the relatively greater weight it attached to the Commonwealth and the United States over Western Europe in its policy of 'concentric circles.' No British Government could ever contemplate submerging Britain's sovereignty within the European movement. On the political front the weak inter-governmental Council of Europe established in 1949 represented the limit to which Britain was willing to go in association with the European movement. In the economic and military spheres, British participation in the EPU and WEU came as the result of considerable pressure, while the rejection of the Schuman

Plan and the EDC, followed by withdrawal from the Messina talks on Euratom and the EEC, all too clearly revealed Britain's determination to avoid any supranational involvement in Western Europe. Thus, far from fulfilling American expectations of vigorous leadership of the European movement, Britain at this stage was not prepared to go beyond limited forms of inter-governmental cooperation with the Continental countries.

American policy during this period suffered from certain inconsistencies which on the whole tended to facilitate the direction of British policy. But the conflicting approaches of the United States and the different roles accorded to Britain at different times were more than a consequence of the difficulty of reconciling the short-term requirements of American Cold War policy with its long-range conceptions. They also stemmed from a basic ambivalence in American attitudes towards Britain. Side by side with the American desire to include Britain in the general framework of European unity, there was always the constant psychological pull of the historical Anglo-American relationship and with it the impulse to treat Britain quite separately from the Continent. This ambivalence, and the underlying uncertainty about the realism of grouping Britain with the Continent, although diminishing rapidly with the progress in the fifties of the supranational European movement never entirely disappeared from American policy. Another aspect of America's ambivalence was the recognition of the importance of Britain's world role in the context of containment, and of the fact that Empire and Commonwealth were bonds which, however repugnant to America economically, nevertheless constituted a buffer to the advance of communism at the periphery of the world, and also acted as important links in the evolution of the Western bloc.

The European movement from 1956 was not without its ironies. After failing to grasp the opportunities for leadership thrust upon her during the forties and fifties, Britain eventually found herself repentantly seeking membership in the EEC only to be faced with the flat rejections of three successive applications, and a prolonged humiliating exclusion during the 1960s from the dynamic new European system emerging on the institutions of the Community and its expanding links of economic association with former European colonies on the African continent. Stripped of its worst supranational features, this development within Western Europe would have fully accorded with the ultimate vision of British policy under Ernest Bevin, who saw in Western Union the consolidation of 'Europe overseas' in the continued service of 'Europe proper', to borrow Lord Strang's apt phraseology.[2] But at the historical crossroads of 1956 Britain under a Conservative Government had not yet adjusted to her postwar decline as a power, and still clinging tenaciously to a traditional world role she lacked the vision necessary for making the leap into the evolving European community centred on the Six. By then, however, the United States no longer had any reservations about Britain's place being properly within a united Western Europe, and from Britain's withdrawal from the preliminary talks at Messina until the British 'change of heart' in the early sixties, Anglo-American relations passed through a particularly cool and restrained phase on the issue of Western European integration. The United States ceased to look to Britain for leadership of the European movement and concentrated on underpinning the efforts of the six continental countries which, five years after their bold initiative in creating the ECSC, were to carry their supranational endeavour to its most far-reaching success in the Rome Treaties of March 1957, establishing Euratom and the EEC.

During this second stage of the European movement, from 1956, the United States was particularly mistrustful of Britain's efforts to promote general interest in an OEEC-wide European free trade area. Coming at a stage when significant progress was being made by the Six towards final agreement on the establishment of the Common Market, this move by Britain was suspected both within the United States and on the Continent as being a grave attempt to subvert interest in the Common Market by posing a weaker alternative arrangement. Preliminary discussions in the OEEC on the proposal for a European free trade area were broken off until the ratification of the Treaty of Rome, since the Six were not prepared to have simultaneous negotiations and wished first and foremost to secure agreement among themselves. When the negotiations were resumed they showed little prospect of success before finally collapsing in November 1958. At that point the so-called 'Outer Seven' comprising Britain, the Scandinavian countries, Switzerland, Austria and Portugal, proceeded to create among themselves the European Free Trade Association (EFTA), established in 1960. American hostility towards the original proposal for a European free trade area was mainly based on the trade 'discrimination' which it would bring without offering the political promise of a supranational united Western Europe contained in the Treaty of Rome, and for which the United States was prepared to suffer some degree of economic discomfort. This attitude also extended to the restricted EFTA and was accompanied by the increasing concern of the United States over the continuing interest of the Seven in reaching early agreement with the Six on some kind of European trading arrangement embracing both these groups. The well known American opposition to any such European arrangement was skilfully exploited by the European Commission in its arguments resisting EFTA entreaties for resumed negotiations for a single European market, which most ardent Europeanists felt would weaken the Community concept and retard its development. In the growing split between Six and Seven on trade relations, on the question of the reform of the OEEC, and on European unity, American interests placed the United States squarely behind the Six on most issues. The result was even further drifting apart between the United States and Britain. The United States did not accept the frequently expounded British thesis that economic division in Western Europe would mean political division, and while the United States was naturally interested in maintaining harmony in Western Europe it was opposed to a multilateral European trading arrangement for a single market and argued that the solution of the trade problems between Six and Seven should be found in a general reduction of tariffs within the GATT. It was principally to forestall any possibility of a coming together of the two groups within a single European market, and to foster the organisation of the major economic powers of the West with a view to coordinating certain aspects of their economic relations with the developing countries, that the United States directly intervened in the impasse between Six and Seven and took the initiative in the establishment of the Development Assistance Group and the transformation of the OEEC into the Organisation for Economic Cooperation and Development (OECD).

Between 1956 and 1961 American and British thinking on Western Europe were constantly at odds, and while openly supporting the Six the United States was moreover particularly determined to play down the Anglo-American relationship. The Suez crisis had marked the nadir of Anglo-American relations, which although improving never managed to repossess the elements of basic interdependence and priority from the American standpoint.

Washington had also come to recognise that Britain's recalcitrant posture on full participation in the European movement was bolstered by a faith in the Anglo-American relationship and the belief that the United States would eventually accept Britain's 'special' position in relation to the Continent. It was the gradual realisation that outside the European Community of the Six she was no longer able to rely on American support for her role in Western Europe, or to claim a 'special relationship', that made Britain develop an increasing sense of isolation based on diminishing influence in Washington and on the European movement. This, compounded with the fear that the new nationalisms of the decolonisation process were casting serious doubts on the possibilities of the Commonwealth as a continuing instrument of British policy, finally forced Britain, in 1961, to make the desperate plunge towards joining the EEC. It was a most welcome change of heart to the United States. For, with the emergence in the early 1960s of President de Gaulle's brand of anti-American Europeanism, and the unparalleled influence which he personally began to throw on the course of the European movement, the United States once again began to look anxiously for British membership in the European Community as a restored bridge for American influence in Western Europe. It was fully a decade, however, before this became a reality, with the successful outcome of the recent negotiations for British entry into the Common Market and Britain's signature on 22 January 1972 of the Treaty of Accession to the European Communities.

Notes

Chapter 1

1 H. S. Truman, *Memoirs*, I ('Year of Decisions'), (London 1955), p. 80.
2 George F. Kennan, *Memoirs, 1925–1950* (London 1968), p. 214.
3 Truman was not in a position to employ force as a means of inducing Russian capitulation to American terms of collaboration:–

> Most of all, I was always aware that there were two enormous land masses that no western army of modern times had ever been able to conquer: Russia and China. It would have been folly... *to attempt to impose our way of life on these huge areas by force!*

> In 1945 and 1946, of all years, such thoughts would have been rejected by the American people before they were even expressed. That was the time when Congressmen in Washington joined in the call to 'get the boys back home'. Truman, *Memoirs*, II, p. 96 – my italics.

For President Truman's 'iron fisted and strong language diplomacy' see his own account: Truman, *Memoirs*, I, p. 492.
4 Kennan, *Memoirs*, pp. 266–7.
5 UNRRA (United Nations Relief and Rehabilitation Administration).
6 Kennan, *Memoirs*, p. 269.
7 F. S. Northedge, *British Foreign Policy, The Process of Readjustment, 1945–1961* (London 1962), p. 41.
8 Kennan, *Memoirs*, p. 258. Kennan's analysis of Potsdam is quite superficial in not taking fully into account the Administration's expectation of an early capitulation of Russia which was a fundamental factor behind the Agreement.
9 Truman, *Memoirs*, I, p. 493.
10 Truman, *Memoirs*, I, pp. 493 and 500.
11 Truman, *Memoirs*, II, p. 117.
12 Truman, *Memoirs*, II, Chapters V and VI, and see p. 97.
13 Truman, *Memoirs*, II, p. 106.
14 Truman, *Memoirs*, II, p. 111.
15 Truman, *Memoirs*, II, p. 112.
16 See, 'President Truman's Special Message to the Congress on Greece and Turkey: The Truman Doctrine, March 12, 1947' in the *Public Papers of the Presidents – Harry S. Truman, 1947*, from the passage beginning 'At the present moment in world history...' See also, Truman, *Memoirs*, II, pp. 111–12. Also, George Ball, *The Discipline*

of Power: Essentials of a modern World Structure (London 1968), p. 299.

17   Truman, *Memoirs*, II, p. 107.

18   According to Ball (*Discipline of Power*, p. 299) containment was merely 'a more sophisticated formulation of the Truman Doctrine'.

19   For Anglo-American economic planning for the postwar world see R. N. Gardner, *Sterling-Dollar Diplomacy, Anglo-American Collaboration in The Reconstruction of Multilateral Trade* (Oxford 1956).

20   Joseph M. Jones, *The Fifteen Weeks* (New York 1955), pp. 255–6.

21   Truman, *Memoirs*, II, p. 120.

22   Northedge, *British Foreign Policy*, p. 44.

23   Papers of Ellen Clayton Garwood: Douglas Enclosure: The Hon. Secretary of State, Washington, 6–25–47, in Aide-Memoire, from Ambassador Lewis Douglas to the Secretary of State, of 27 June 1947. (Correspondence of Mrs Garwood, Box 1.) My italics.

24   Truman, *Memoirs*, II, p. 122.

25   It should be noted that it was initially contemplated by the Policy Planning Staff that the initiative for a European recovery programme might first be sought through the United Nations Economic Commission for Europe. But the view was expressed in the Policy Planning Staff's paper of 23 May that the offer should be put in such a way that the Eastern European countries would 'either exclude themselves by unwillingness to accept the proposed conditions or agree to abandon the exclusive orientation of their economies'. (Kennan, *Memoirs*, p. 341, quoted therein from the 23 May Paper.) This was precisely the Bevin-Bidault approach to Russia. According to one commentator, 'While it may be inaccurate to accuse the (British) Foreign Secretary of having intrigued to keep Russia out . . . Bevin must have breathed a sigh of relief to hear that Stalin could not go along with the two Western Powers' (Northedge, *British Foreign Policy*, p. 44). Of further interest is Harold Callender's column in the *New York Times*, 1 July 1947.

26   As quoted in Northedge, *British Foreign Policy*, p. 43. Northedge however, contends that 'it is fairly certain [that this explanation] was not genuine.' Unfortunately, he fails to say why he thinks it was not.

27   Truman, *Memoirs*, II, p. 122.

28   Interview.

29   The Russians hoped to gain their objectives by having an American representative attend the plenary conference, in which the calculation and allocation of Marshall aid would be decided by majority view, which it was hoped would bind the Americans by virtue of their presence.

30   Interview.

31 One such case is Louis J. Halle, *The Cold War as History* (New York 1967). However, even Halle himself concedes: 'When I found myself writing a history of the Cold War . . . I had to face the fact that my nominal subject was not a physical fact of nature, with the definition proper to such facts. This did not mean that I was free to define it so as to include, let us say, the Boer War, since there was a consensus on what the term referred to that I had to respect. Nevertheless, there was still wide latitude for definition within the consensus, and so I fixed, as the beginning of the Cold War, Moscow's decision to oppose the Marshall Plan in June 1947. . . The arbitrariness of these limits was obvious. . . .' (Louis J. Halle, 'A Multitude of Cold Wars', *International Journal, Canadian Institute of International Affairs*, XXIII, No. 3, Summer 1968, p. 336).

32 Kennan, *Memoirs*, p. 325. See also, Truman, *Memoirs*, II, p. 118.

33 Kennan, *Memoirs*, Chapter 14, for the views of the PPS.

34 Garwood Papers: Marshall Plan Project – Oral History Research Office – Colombia University, 1962. Interview with Dean Acheson, p. 4.

35 See the quotation from the Aide-Memoire on the Anglo-American talks, p. 20. See also Kennan, *Memoirs*, Chapter 14, and bearing in mind that Marshall returned from Moscow 'shaken by the realization of the seriousness and urgency of the plight of *Western* Europe' (p. 325), note especially the extracts quoted from various papers of the Policy Planning Staff, in which the reference is consistently to 'Western Europe', or to 'Europe' really implying Western Europe. For example: 'This European program must envisage bringing Western Europe to a point . . .', quoted on p. 337. Another conspicuous example is in the following passage which, according to Kennan, 'later found its way, almost verbatim, into General Marshall's Harvard speech'. The brackets used in the passage referred to by Kennan are my own to indicate the terms omitted in the Harvard Address, and the passage is as follows: 'It would be neither fitting nor efficacious for this Government to undertake to draw up unilaterally [and to promulgate formally on its own initiative] a program designed to place [Western] Europe on its feet economically.' See p. 336.

36 Truman, *Memoirs*, II, p. 119. It should be noted that although Truman refers to 'the nations of Europe' the construction and sense of his sentence clearly indicate Western Europe.

37 Evidenced, for instance, by Assistant Secretary of State Clayton's reasoning: 'Europe is steadily deteriorating. The political position reflects the economic . . . Without further prompt and substantial aid from the United States, economic, social and political disintegration will overwhelm Europe. Aside from the awful implications which this would have for the future peace and security of

K

the world, the immediate effects on our domestic economy would be disastrous: markets for our surplus production gone, unemployment, depression, a heavily unbalanced budget on the background of a mountainous war debt. *These things must not happen . . . The United States must run this show.*' Papers of William L. Clayton: 'The European Crisis' (31 May 1947: Confidential Marshall Plan Memos: General File, Box 42). My italics.

38 Interview.

39 Interviews.

40 Truman, *Memoirs*, II, p. 122.

41 *The Journals of David E. Lilienthal, II, The Atomic Energy Years, 1945–1950* (New York 1964), p. 329.

42 The creation of the post of US Special Representative in Europe, and the appointment of Harriman, might well have been to counterbalance the Republican pressure on Executive appointments, and the fact that most of the ECA positions had been filled by Republican preferences (*Lilienthal Journals*, p. 337). In the event, however, the integrationist lead of Hoffman and his industrious attachment to his task received full support from the Administration.

43 See Chapter 3.

44 Jones, *The Fifteen Weeks* pp. 200–1, 204–5, 242–53.

45 Kennan, *Memoirs*, p. 337.

46 Kennan, *Memoirs*, p. 337.

47 *Britain and the United States, problems in co-operation – a Joint report by study groups of The Council on Foreign Relations, New York, and the Royal Institute of International Affairs* by H. L. Roberts and P. A. Wilson, (London 1953), p. 116. For the pre-1947 interest of the United States in European Unity, see Max Beloff, *The United States and the Unity of Europe* (London 1963).

48 *The Christian Science Monitor*, 14 November 1947. Dulles, who accompanied Secretary Marshall to the Moscow Conference of Foreign Ministers, March-April 1947, had raised there the subject of a possible continental economic unity of Europe supported by the United States, Britain, France, and Russia, as a solution to the German problem. (J. F. Dulles' Papers: Dulles to Charles Edmundson, letter of 20 May 1947: 11. Correspondence 1945–7, Folder 1947 (1).) See also Dulles to Geoffrey Parsons, letter of 6 February 1947 (Ibid).

49 The Mutual Security of 1951 (Sec. 101 (a)) was even more explicit in stating among its aims 'the economic unification and political federation of Europe'.

50 Including among others – Senators J. W. Fulbright, E. D. Thomas, B. McMahon, T. F. Green, A. H. Vandenberg, H. C. Lodge, Jr., Alexander Wiley, J. W. Sparkman, as well as Representatives Boggs, W. Judd, K. Keating, and H. Ellsworth.

51 Acheson as reported in the *Manchester Guardian*, 10 February 1949.
52 Text of Secretary Acheson's testimony on the 'Extension of the European Recovery Programme', in the *New York Times*, 22 February 1950. Secretary Marshall was of the same view and said much the same thing while giving his sympathy to the Fulbright Resolution (21 March 1947): see *Britain and the United States*, Roberts and Wilson, p. 116.
53 Letter from the Hon. Howard Bruce to the Hon. H. Alexander Smith, in *Congressional Record*, 81st Congress, 1st Session (1949), p. 5297.
54 See, 'Hearings before the Committee on Foreign Relations, US Senate, 81st Congress, 1st Session, on S.833', February 1949, 'Extension of European Recovery', p. 85. See also *The Times*, 12 February 1949.

Chapter 2

1 Beloff, *The United States and the Unity of Europe* (London 1963), p. 21.
2 See Beloff, *The United States and the Unity of Europe*, p. 21; and Kennan, *Memoirs*, pp. 406–7, where he refers to his support of the 'dumb-bell' concept. Kennan in fact was thinking more along the lines of Churchill's 'English-speaking' alliance as one pillar of Atlantic community, with continental European unity as the other.
3 Kennan, *Memoirs*, p. 455.
4 H. C. Allen, *Great Britain and the United States*, *A History of Anglo-American Relations* (*1783–1952*) (London 1954), p. 781.
5 On the revival of the Anglo-American alliance, see Chapter 4.
6 Dalton's Diary, 15 October 1948.
7 Dalton's Diary, 15 September 1948.
8 See for instance Kennan, *Memoirs*, p. 323.
9 HC Debates, 5th Series, 446, c. 388 (22 January 1948).
10 This spheres of influence approach is indisputably clear in Bevin's foreign policy address before the House of Commons, of 22 January 1948. HC Debates, 5th Series, 446.
11 Dalton's Diary, 15 October 1948.
12 Dalton's Diary, 17 November 1948.
13 It should be noted that the intention to continue exploitation of Africa was shared by some of the continental countries. According to Northedge (in *British Foreign Policy*, pp. 166–7): 'Moreover, the Europe of the Six, as Schuman's reference to the development of Africa in the original outline of his plan showed, tended to regard the new world emerging from European colonialism rather as a prospect for European enterprise than as a birthplace of free and equal states.' The author, however, continued in a vein that tends to acquit Britain of such motives before concluding that 'at any rate' it 'was the fear of liberal-minded British people' that Britain 'might have found herself committed to the support of these policies'.

Ironically, it is Northedge's implied suggestion that Britain's aloofness from the Europe of the Six and her continued attachment to the Commonwealth lay partly in the intention of the Six to treat emergent states 'as a prospect for European enterprise'.

14 HC Debates, 5th Series, 446 (1948), cc. 398–9 and 402. (My italics.)

15 Ernest Bevin, HC Debates, 5th Series, 450 (1947–8), c. 110, speech of 4 May 1948.

16 Signed by Britain, France, Belgium, Luxembourg and the Netherlands for collective defence, and economic, social, and cultural collaboration.

17 HC Debates, 5th Series, 450 (1947–8), c. 1108; speech of 4 May 1948.

18 Dalton's Diary, 17 November 1948.

19 J. F. Dulles Papers: Copy of memo. of 27 April 1948, of secret meeting at Blair House between Secretary Marshall, Under-Secretary Lovett, Senator Vandenberg, and J. F. Dulles with reference to the possible North Atlantic Treaty. – 1. Writings . . . of J. F. D.; G. Notes and Memoranda 1917–49; File, 1948. It should be noted that much of the same argument served to expedite military aid to Western Europe. See for instance Bevin's indication to Marshall that without military Lend Lease Western Europe would go Communist as reported by Dalton, in Dalton's Diary 15 October 1948. Related to this is Dulles' statement of 22 October 1948, that 'Marshall shares my view that sense of total military insecurity is at the root of many troubles and current meeting here of ECA confirms that it is threatening to undermine European Recovery Plan. Marshall thinks we have the arms to equip French divisions . . .' in J. F. Dulles Papers: Confirmation Copy, US Mission, New York, For Dewey, Number 11, 22 October 1948, 11.30.11 Correspondence, 1948–9, File 1948 (2).

20 See Chapter 4.

21 Kennan, *Memoirs*, p. 359.

22 In his apologetic on the 'X-Article', Kennan, in his *Memoirs*, attempts to convince his reader that 'the "containment" of which I was speaking was not something that I thought we could, necessarily, do everywhere successfully, or even need to do everywhere successfully. . . .' He does confess, however, that 'why this was not made clear in the X-Article is, again, a mystery'. Kennan, *Memoirs*, p. 359.

23 *Congressional Record, Appendix*, 81st Congress, 1st Session, p. A5690 (7 September 1949).

24 Dulles Papers: Notes for Foreign Policy Discussions (8/21/52); Writings, G. Notes and Memoranda, 1950–9, Folder, 1952.

25 Truman, *Memoirs*, I, p. 460.

26 Interview.

27 See for instance, Ball, *Discipline of Power*, pp. 298–9.

28 Although largely on account of the idiosyncrasies of Gaullist diplomacy, the American Grand Design has not yet attained its perfect form (a 'dumb-bell' Atlantic Community), this in itself has been of little consequence to the position of the majority of 'developing' countries which still find themselves orbiting around the metropolitan North Atlantic grouping. See for instance, Pierre Jalee, *The Pillage of the Third World* (New York, 1968), and of special interest is the point of view on p. 13.

29 Notably, the Consultative Assembly was formally prevented from discussing defence.

30 Lord Strang recalls (*Home and Abroad*, p. 290) that 'When the Council of Europe was first mooted, [Bevin] is reported to have burst out: "I don't like it. I don't like it. When you open that Pandora's box, you will find it full of Trojan horses." '

31 Dulles Papers: 'Confirmation Copy of Dulles to Dewey, Number 21, 13 October 1948':– 11 Correspondence, 1948–9, File 1948 (2).

32 Dalton's Diary, 24 January 1950. The suggestion came from Sir Stafford Cripps and was endorsed by the Cabinet.

33 See Chapter 6.

34 See Chapter 3.

35 See Chapter 5.

36 Churchill's speeches at Zurich (19 September 1946), and at the Hague Congress (7 May 1948) were generally misinterpreted as a declaration in favour of British participation in European unity.

Chapter 3

1 For a detailed study of Anglo-American planning for the postwar economic order, see R. N. Gardner, *Sterling-Dollar Diplomacy, Anglo-American Collaboration In The Reconstruction Of Multilateral Trade* (Oxford 1956).

2 Gardner, *Sterling-Dollar Diplomacy*, Chapter XVII.

3 Gardner, *Sterling-Dollar Diplomacy*, Chapters III, IV, XII.

4 Gardner, *Sterling-Dollar Diplomacy*, Chapter X.

5 Remarks of Paul G. Hoffman before OEEC in Paris, July 1948.

6 Papers of William L. Clayton: 'The European Crisis' (31 May 1947: Confidential Marshall Plan Memos: General File, Box 42).

7 Dalton's Diary; 27 June 1947.

8 Papers of Ellen Clayton Garwood: Aide-Memoires: Douglas Enclosure – The Hon. Secretary of State, Washington, 6–25–47. (Folder: Correspondence of Mrs Garwood; Box 1).

9 Gardner, *Sterling-Dollar Diplomacy*, Chapter X.

10 No greater testimony of this is needed than the terms of the loan and the atmosphere in which it was negotiated, see Gardner, *Sterling-Dollar Diplomacy*.

11 Dalton's Diary: 28 July 1947.
12 Dulles Papers: Dulles to Mr Ivor Thomas, letter of 22 August 1947.
     (11. Correspondence 1945–7, Folder 1947 (2).)
13 Gardner, *Sterling-Dollar Diplomacy*, p. 317.
14 Dulles Papers: Memorandum of Conversations at State Department,
     30 March 1950. (1. Writings: G. Notes and Memoranda, 1950–9:
     Folder, 1950.)
15 'Extension of European Recovery' – Hearings Before the Committee
     on Foreign Relations, United States Senate, 81st Congress, 1st
     Session, on s.833, February 1949, p. 130.
16 See Howard S. Ellis, *The Economics of Freedom, The Progress and
     Future of Aid to Europe* (New York 1950), pp. 374–5.
17 William Diebold, Jr., *Trade and Payments in Western Europe, A Study
     in Economic Cooperation 1947–1951* (New York 1952), p. 19.
18 Diebold, *Trade and Payments in Western Europe*, Chapter III.
19 The complex issue of drawing rights involved a procedure of prior
     bilateral negotiation on the anticipated liability at the end of a year
     of one trading partner to the other. The debtor country would
     receive as a 'gift' his anticipated deficit, which constituted his
     drawing rights on the creditor, provided the debtor had exhausted
     his 'existing resources' in the creditor's currency. The creditor
     country received in turn 'conditional aid' from the ECA, but on
     the basis of its overall dollar deficit. Under the agreement drawing
     rights could only be used against the country to which it originally
     referred in the bilateral negotiations. According to the revised
     Agreement, up to thirty-five per cent of a country's drawing rights
     could be transferred and used against any other country, provided
     again that the country exercising the drawing rights had exhausted
     its holdings of the other country's currency. For details on this
     issue and the workings of the Agreement, see Diebold, Chapters
     III & IV.
20 See below.
21 Diebold, *Trade and Payments in Western Europe*, p. 169.
22 Diebold, *Trade and Payments in Western Europe*, p. 178.
23 In both cases this was approximately twenty-five per cent. (Diebold,
     Trade and Payments in Western Europe, p. 182.) Some attempt is
     made by Diebold to analyse the real expansion of intra-European
     trade resulting from quota reductions (pp. 181–5).
24 Diebold, *Trade and Payments in Western Europe*, Chapter XII.
25 Diebold, *Trade and Payments in Western Europe*.
26 Truman Papers: Hoffman to Truman, letter of 21 September 1950
     (Series: 462L (1950) – 4261 (Misc.), Box No. 1282).
27 Ellis, *The Economics of Freedom*, p. 47.
28 *The Times*, 9 February 1949.
29 *The Times*, 9 February 1949, quoted above.

30 Diebold, *Trade and Payments in Western Europe*, p. 160.
31 See above, footnote 19, p. 142, for compromise on transferability.
32 See above, p. 42–3.
33 Diebold, *Trade and Payments in Western Europe*, p. 161.
34 Ellis, *The Economics of Freedom*, p. 314.
35 For a detailed comparison see 'The Proposed European Payments Union', *Congressional Record* – Senate, 81st Congress, 2nd Session (Pt. 7, Vol. 96), pp. 8716–9: and see also Diebold, *Trade and Payments in Western Europe*.
36 Each participating country was allocated a 'quota' apprxoimating to fifteen per cent of its trade and payments with all the other members in 1949.
37 The extent of credit from the EPU operated on a sliding scale: the debtor received full credit from the EPU for a deficit of up to twenty per cent of its quota; for the next twenty per cent it was required to pay four per cent in gold or dollars with the remaining sixteen per cent as credit; on the third twenty per cent the proportion was eight per cent in gold or dollars and twelve per cent credit and so on. A similar sliding scale with different proportions applied to payment by the EPU of creditors (first twenty per cent = nil; and for each of the remaining four twenty per cent stages ten per cent would be credited to account with the EPU and ten per cent paid by the EPU to the creditor in gold or dollars). For full details see Diebold, *Trade and Payments in Western Europe*, pp. 92–5.
38 'The Proposed European Payments Union', p. 8717.
39 'The Proposed European Payments Union'. This council comprised representatives from the Treasury, Department of State, Commerce, Federal Reserve, Export-Import Bank, and ECA.
40 'The Proposed European Payments Union', p. 8718.
41 'The Proposed European Payments Union'.
42 'The Proposed European Payments Union'.
43 Diebold, *Trade and Payments in Western Europe*, p. 90.
44 See Diebold, *Trade and Payments in Western Europe*, p. 100.
45 'The Proposed European Payments Union', p. 8718.
46 477 HC Debates, 5s., 11 July 1950, col. 1144.
47 Diebold, *Trade and Payments in Western Europe*, p. 88.
48 'Britain and the United States, Problems in Cooperation', *A Joint Report of the Council on Foreign Relations and the Royal Institute of International Affairs* (RIIA, 1953), p. 137.
49 Quoted in Diebold, *Trade and Payments in Western Europe*, p. 91, from US House of Representatives, Hearings before the Committee on Foreign Affairs, 81st Congress, 2nd Session, on H.R. 7378 (Washington, 1950). Part I, II, 72, 73.

50   Diebold, *Trade and Payments in Western Europe.*
51   See Chapter 5.
52   Diebold, *Trade and Payments in Western Europe*, p. 90.
53   Diebold, *Trade and Payments in Western Europe*, p. 101.
54   Diebold, *Trade and Payments in Western Europe*, pp. 101–2.
55   Diebold, *Trade and Payments in Western Europe*, p. 103.
56   Diebold, *Trade and Payments in Western Europe*, pp. 105–6.
57   *Congressional Record* – Senate, 80th Congress, 2nd Session, 3 March
     1948 (Vol. 94, Pt. 2), pp. 2030–1.
58   'The Great Design', from the St Louis *Post Dispatch* of 24 February
     1948, as read into the *Congressional Record* by Senator J. W.
     Fulbright, *ibid.*, p. 2039.
59   *Congressional Record* – House, 80th Congress, 2nd Session (94, Pt. 3),
     March 1948, p. 4067.
60   *Congressional Record* – House, March 1968, p. 4067.
61   *Congressional Record*, March 1948. Cf. Remarks of Ernest Bevin
     before the House of Commons (22 January 1948) as quoted on pp.
     24–5 above.
62   Representative Powell, *Congressional Record*, March 1948.
63   As quoted in 'The Great Design' from the St Louis *Post Dispatch* of
     24 February 1948.
64   Rep. Powell, *Congressional Record*, March 1948.
65   *Hansard*, 460 HC Debates, 5s., (28 January 1949), col. 1251.
66   *Hansard*, 460 HC Debates (28 January 1949), columns 1251–2.
67   Quoted in *The Times*, 9 February 1949.
68   Dalton's Diary, 15 June 1949.
69   Dalton's Diary, 15 June 1949, and also 1 July 1949.
70   Dalton's Diary, 15 June 1949 and 1 July 1949.
71   See Dalton's reporting on Acheson's attitude – Dalton's Diary of
     1 July 1949.
72   Dalton's Diary, 1 July 1949.
73   Kennan, *Memoirs*, p. 458.
74   Kennan, *Memoirs*, p. 461.
75   See Dalton's Diary, 1 July 1949.
76   Kennan, *Memoirs*, p. 459.
77   'We Must Aid Britain', Remarks of Hon. Hubert Humphrey for the
     Congressional Record, Appendix, 81st Congress, 1st Session
     (7 September 1949), p. A5690.
78   See Kennan, *Memoirs*, p. 462.
79   Kennan, *Memoirs*, p. 462.
80   Roberts and Wilson, *Britain and the United States, Problems in Co-
     operation*, p. 140.
81   Ray Cromley, 'Merger With United Kingdom?', *Wall Street Journal*,
     16 August 1949, as quoted in the *Congressional Record*, Appendix,
     81st Congress, 1st Session, pp. A5348–9.

82   Ray Cromley, 'Merger With United Kingdom?'
83   See Chapter 2.
84   Kennan, *Memoirs*, pp. 459–60.
85   Kennan, *Memoirs*, p. 459.
86   Kennan, *Memoirs*, p. 462n.
87   Kennan, *Memoirs*, pp. 461–2. (My italics.)
88   Kennan, *Memoirs*, pp. 407, 460, 462.
89   See Kennan, *Memoirs*, pp. 426–7, 465 ff., on relations with Acheson
     and on difficulties of Policy Planning Staff having direct access to
     the Secretary of State.
90   *Financial Times*, 18 August 1949. See also, *Manchester Guardian* and
     The Daily Telegraph of same date.
91   The Mutual Security Act of 1951, Report to accompany H.R. 5113
     (Senate – Calendar No. 678, Report No. 703, 82nd Congress,
     1st Session), p. 24.
92   See Chapter 5.
93   See Chapter 5.
94   Harold Callender, 'Six European Lands to Speed Meeting of Re-
     sources Pool', *New York Times*, 3 June 1950, as quoted in the
     Congressional Record, 81st Congress, 2nd Session, p. 8099.
95   *Congressional Record*, 81st Congress, 2nd Session, p. 9122.

Chapter 4

1   Lord Ismay, *NATO – The First Five Years, 1949–1954*, p. 8.
2   The Inter-American Treaty of Reciprocal Assistance (Treaty of Rio
    de Janeiro of 2 September 1947).
3   Truman, *Memoirs*, II, p. 256.
4   Dulles Papers: Item C – Copy of memo of 27 April 1948, of secret
    meeting at Blair House between Secretary Marshall, Under-
    Secretary Lovett, Senator Vandenberg, and J. F. Dulles, with
    reference to the possible North Atlantic Treaty. Robert A. Lovett
    succeeded Acheson as Under-Secretary of State on 1 July 1947.
5   Dulles Papers: Memorandum of 27 April 1948.
6   Dulles Papers: Memorandum of 27 April 1948.
7   Geoffrey L. Goodwin, *Britain and the United Nations* (London 1957),
    pp. 56–7.
8   Dulles Papers: Memorandum of 27 April 1948.
9   Ismay, *NATO*, p. 9.
10 Ismay, *NATO*, p. 7.
11 HC Debates, 5th Series, Vol. 450, cc. 1110–11 (1948).
12 Truman, *Memoirs*, II, p. 259. (My italics.)
13 Opinion polls revealed a precipitous decline in the popularity of both
    the Democratic Party and the President. In the spring of 1948,
    Truman's popularity 'hit an all-time-low' of thirty-two per cent as

against seventy per cent at his succession to the Presidency. (See Truman, *Memoirs*, II, p. 188.) There was also a visible splintering of the Democratic Party among supporters of Truman, the Wallace Progressives, and the Dixiecrats. Although a fair degree of co-operation was solicited from the Republicans on foreign policy, this was mainly due to the influence of Sen. A. H. Vandenberg, and the Administration's policies were consistently under attack from the isolationist wing of the Republicans, mainly from the influential Senators Taft (Ohio), Wherry, and Hickenlooper. The Executive was forced to concede a substantial degree of control in foreign policy to the Republicans, whose control of Congress invited 'bipartisanship', the recipe of which was, according to Senator Vandenberg, 'the reciprocal need for "team ball" (calling) for maximum co-operation at both ends of the avenue in searching for a final, unified foreign policy.' Dulles Papers: Letter from A. H. Vandenberg to Hon. Homer Ferguson, 31 May 1950. (II. Correspondence, 1950, Folder January – May, 1950 (1))

14   See for instance, Truman, *Memoirs*, II, p. 259.

15   It should be noted that this consideration had recently weighed most heavily on the State Department's planning for the Marshall Plan. See Kennan, *Memoirs*, pp. 338–40.

16   Truman, *Memoirs*, II. p. 259.

17   Senate Resolution 239, 80th Congress, 2nd Session, 11 June 1948, paragraph 3. In reiterating the fundamental principles of American aid to Western Europe, this paragraph of the Vandenberg Resolution carefully provided the type of reassurance which Congress and the American public would anxiously seek when the time came for an alliance, or later, for military aid.

18   Dean Acheson, *Present at the Creation* (New York 1969), p. 397.

19   See Chapters 6 and 7 on the EDC and WEU.

20   See Acheson, *Present at the Creation*, pp. 435–40.

21   Dean Acheson succeeded Marshall as Secretary of State in January 1949 and was the Administration's pilot for the North Atlantic Treaty through Congress.

22   See Chapter 6.

23   Truman, *Memoirs*, II, pp. 270–1.

24   'US Bases in Britain', in *The World Today* (OUP), August 1960, 60, No. 8.

25   H. C. Allen, *Great Britain and the United States, A History of Anglo-American Relations (1783–1952)* (London 1954).

26   Winston Churchill to Eisenhower, letter of 1 July 1948, in Eisenhower Papers – Personal Files Of General Of The Army Dwight D. Eisenhower, 1916–1952.

27 Eisenhower to Pug (General Sir Hastings Ismay), letter of 1 July 1948, in Eisenhower Papers – Personal Files Of General Of The Army Dwight D. Eisenhower, 1916–1952.

28 H. G. Nicholas, 'Britain and the United States', (London 1963), p. 64.

Chapter 5

1 See for instance Dalton's Diary: End of 1948 (2) and 9 February 1951.

2 Dalton's Diary of 9 February 1951.

3 Dulles Papers: Memorandum of Conversation between Secretary Acheson and Mr Dulles, 14 February 1949: 1. Writings; G. Notes and Memoranda, 1917–49: Folder – 1949. Little wonder that Kennan's Policy Planning Staff could get no direct indication from Acheson and other senior members of the Administration as to whether the American Government 'really wished to proceed along [the] line' of putting forward a proposal in the interest of German unity which offered some possibility of acceptance by the Russians during the Berlin Blockade. See Kennan, *Memoirs*, pp. 421–2.

4 For details on the London Programme see Kennan, *Memoirs*, Chapter 18; and Adenauer, *Memoirs, 1945–1953* (London 1965), Chapter 7.

5 Committee of European Economic Cooperation, July-September 1947, I, General Report, HMSO 1947, p. 39, as quoted in F. S. Northedge, *British Foreign Policy*, p. 79. Further to the point, on 21 July 1947, Dulles wrote to Sen. A. H. Vandenberg that: 'In Europe some economic unity is imperative. That economic unity, if it is to be self-supporting, will have to depend largely upon the revival of the Ruhr, and that in turn requires first a political solution. The French will never go along with that, and if we try to force a revival of Germany before some political solution on the Ruhr. . . the French will balk and probably be thrown back into the hands of the Russians.' In Dulles Papers; 11. Correspondence 1945–7, Folder 1947 (2).

6 See Northedge, *British Foreign Policy*, pp. 86–94.

7 See Northedge, *British Foreign Policy*.

8 Kennan, *Memoirs*, pp. 445–6.

9 Adenauer, *Memoirs*, pp. 208 ff.

10 See Chapter 4.

11 See for instance Adenauer, *Memoirs*, pp. 267–9.

12 See for instance Richard Mayne, *The Community of Europe* (London 1962), pp. 87–8.

13 Adenauer, *Memoirs*, p. 202.

14 William Diebold, Jr., *The Schuman Plan, A Study in Economic Co-operation 1950–1959* (New York 1959), p. 1.

15 Reported by Adenauer, *Memoirs*, p. 257.

16 Mayne, *The Community of Europe*, pp. 90–1

17   As quoted in Diebold, *The Schuman Plan*, p. 1.

18   Adenauer, *Memoirs*, pp. 256–7.

19   In the announcement of the Schuman Plan, only France and Germany were specifically referred to, the 'other' European countries being invited to participate.

20   The available literature on the subject is quite unsatisfactory in this regard. The tendency has been to attribute the British negative simply to Britain's jealous guard over her sovereignty, in relation to the plan itself and to the prospect of future British participation in European federation, without examination of the impact of the plan on the direction of Bevin's diplomacy. It has also been suggested that the British Government 'was not unhappy that the French stipulation [of acceptance of supranational principle as a pre-condition to negotiations] had provided a good issue for staying out of the negotiations' (Diebold, *The Schuman Plan*, p. 57) and that in Britain 'the Schuman Plan was not taken seriously' (Ulrich Sahm, 'Britain and Europe, 1950', in *International Affairs*, January 1967, 43, No. 1, p. 21). But if these allegations were true, it is difficult to account for the tedious efforts of the British Government to have the Six give way on the question of prior acceptance of the supranational principle.

21   Apart from there being only the slightest forewarning to the British Government, Bevin was seriously ill.

22   On these discussions see *The Times*, 10 May 1950.

23   *New York Times*, 8 May 1950.

24   It should also be mentioned that it was no mere coincidence that Bevin and Acheson issued no statement at all after their discussions – see *The Times*, 10 May 1950.

25   As quoted in Sahm, 'Britain and Europe 1950', p. 16.

26   The Labour Party, 'European Unity' (London 1950).

27   Dalton's Diary, 15 June 1950.

28   Dalton's Diary, 16 June 1950.

29   See for instance: Alastair Cooke, 'All America Angry With Labour', *Manchester Guardian*, 15 June 1950; 'Mr Attlee Under Fire In US on Labour Manifesto', *The Times*, 18 June 1950; 'Labour Pamphlet A Shock To US', *The Times*, 19 June 1950; 'Key Senators Ask Attlee To Explain', *New York Times*, 16 June 1950.

30   *Financial Times*, 22 June 1950. The *Financial Times* dismissed the proposal with the view that 'the most charitable description of the proposal is that it originates out of an excess of goodwill in favour of European integration'. Acheson had earlier resisted such pressure from a Congressional minority – see *New York Times*, 8 June 1950.

31   The *Yorkshire Post*, 5 June 1950.

32 Harold Callender, 'Six European Lands To Speed Meeting Of Resources Pool', as quoted in the *Congressional Record*, 81st Congress, 2nd Session, 1950, p. 8098.
33 *Congressional Record*, 81st Congress, 2nd Session, 1950, p. 6887.
34 *The Times*, 6 June 1950.
35 *New York Times*, 5 June 1950.
36 Reported in *The Times*, 6 June 1950.
37 To this extent the American attitude corresponded very much to the French. (See Sahm, 'Britain and Europe, 1950'.) However, Sahm seems to be arguing that it was not the French intention that the British participate in the negotiations (particularly pp. 16–18), and in the comment following the article Younger remarks: 'We know that the plan itself was serious, but the proposal that Britain should join it probably was not.' (p. 25). No satisfactory evidence is produced anywhere in the article to show that the French did not intend or desire that Britain should participate in the negotiations. The evidence on the whole tends to point to the fact that the French had little reason to expect that Britain would accept the supranational principle in order to participate in the negotiations. But it hardly follows from this that the French did not hope or intend that Britain should join the negotiations on the Schuman Plan. The proposed ECSC stripped of the supranational principle would have made little sense to the French, and the French position was not that they did not intend Britain to join the negotiations but that they had to choose between ensuring the supranational principle at risk of British non-participation in the negotiations or having British participation at grave risk to the supranational principle.
38 *New York Times*, 5 June 1950.
39 *New York Times*, 2 December 1951.
40 Conference of Strasbourg between delegations of the Congress of the United States of America and of the Consultative Assembly of the Council of Europe, Official Record of Debates, Strasbourg, 19–23 November 1951 (Secretariat-General of the Council of Europe).

Chapter 6

1 For details of the Pleven proposal see Adenauer, *Memoirs*, pp. 345–6.
2 Northedge, *British Foreign Policy*, p. 153.
3 Truman, *Memoirs*, II, pp. 268 ff.
4 Adenauer, *Memoirs*, p. 345.
5 Adenauer, *Memoirs*, pp. 407–8.
6 Adenauer, *Memoirs*, p. 353.
7 Adenauer, *Memoirs*, p. 347.
8 Reported, Adenauer, *Memoirs*, p. 347.
9 Adenauer, *Memoirs*, p. 358.

10 Truman, *Memoirs*, II, p. 276.
11 The Washington Declaration is cited and its meaning carefully analysed in 'The Union Of Europe: Its Progress, Problems, Prospects, And Place in the Western World' (Council of Europe – Strasbourg – October 1951), pp. 41 ff.
12 Sir Anthony Eden, *The Memoirs of the Rt. Hon. Sir Anthony Eden, K.G., P.C., M.C. – Full Circle* (London 1960), p. 33.
13 Eden, Gabriel Silver Lecture, at Columbia University, 11 January 1952: as quoted in Eden, *Memoirs*, p. 36.
14 Eden, *Memoirs*, pp. 32 and 34.
15 D. D. Eisenhower, *The White House Years – Mandate For Change 1953–1956* (London 1963), pp. 405 and 246.
16 Adenauer, *Memoirs*, p. 348.
17 See Chapter 4.
18 Truman, *Memoirs*, II, p. 274.
19 Truman, *Memoirs*, pp. 274–5.
20 *The Times*, 23 January 1952. (My italics.)
21 Quoted in Dalton's Diary, 19 December 1951.
22 General D. D. Eisenhower, Address to the English Speaking Union, London, 3 July 1951, as quoted by Edward A. Conway, 'Eisenhower and European Union', Appendix to the *Congressional Record*, 82nd Congress, 1st Session (1951), p. A5633.
23 Eden, *Memoirs*, p. 35.
24 Eden, *Memoirs*, p. 40.
25 Truman, *Memoirs*, II, p. 276.
26 *New York Herald Tribune*, 28 August 1951.
27 Theodore Geiger and H. Van B. Cleveland, 'Making Western Europe Defensible – An appraisal of the Effectiveness of United States Policy in Western Europe', NPA, Planning Pamphlets No. 74, August 1951.
28 *New York Herald Tribune*, 28 August 1951.
29 Beardsley Ruml, 'The United States of Europe: A Hope for Peace', *Collier's Magazine*, 21 June 1952 – Extension of Remarks by the Hon. John W. McCormack, of Massachusetts, in Appendix to the *Congressional Record*, 82nd Congress, 2nd Session, p. A3849.
30 *New York Times*, 19 December 1952.
31 Eden, *Memoirs*, p. 33.
32 Eisenhower, *The White House Years*, p. 398.
33 Eisenhower Papers: Eisenhower to Eden, letter of 5 February 1952; in Personal Files of General of the Army Dwight D. Eisenhower, 1916–52.
34 HC Debates, 495, 5th Series, c. 820–1.
35 Joint Communiqué, 9 January 1952, as printed in the *Congressional Record*, 82nd Congress, 2nd Session, 1942, p. 1205.
36 HC Debates, 495, 5th Series, c. 876, February 1952.

37 Truman, *Memoirs*, II, p. 276.
38 Eisenhower as quoted in Truman, *Memoirs*, II, p. 198.
39 Truman, *Memoirs*, p. 530.
40 Dulles Papers: Dulles to General Eisenhower, letter of 20 May 1952: 11. Correspondence, 1952–1954; Folder, March–December, 1952 (2).
41 Truman, *Memoirs*, II, p. 455.
42 Truman, *Memoirs*, II, p. 531.
43 See for instance General Eisenhower's reaction to an invitation from President Truman for a briefing on the situation in the White House (letters between President Truman and General Eisenhower, in Truman, *Memoirs*, II, pp. 542–3); and the controversy over the General's withdrawal of a tribute to General Marshall from a speech to be delivered in Wisconsin during the election campaign, for which Eisenhower was subsequently accused of having capitulated to the McCarthyites (for Truman's account see Truman, *Memoirs*, pp. 531–2; for Eisenhower's, see Eisenhower, *The White House Years*, p. 318).
44 Eisenhower, *The White House Years*, p. 86.
45 Eisenhower, *The White House Years*, p. 142.
46 Eisenhower, *The White House Years*, p. 142.
47 R. Drummond and G. Coblentz, *Duel at the Brink* (New York 1960), p. 25, and see Chap. 11. See also A. H. Berding, *Dulles on Diplomacy* (Princeton 1965), pp. 14–15: and Sherman Adams, *Firsthand Report – The Story of the Eisenhower Administration* (New York 1961), Chap. 6.
48 Dulles Papers: Dulles to Kenneth de Courcy, letter of 28 February 1952: 11. Correspondence 1952–54; Folder – January–February, 1952 (1).
49 Eisenhower, *The White House Years*, pp. 140–1.
50 See above, p. 103.
51 An example being Eisenhower's request for Congressional approval to the use the Armed Forces to protect Formosa in 1955 – see Sherman Adams, *Firsthand Report*, p. 129.
52 Eisenhower, *The White House Years*, pp. 192, 194–5, 199, 201.
53 See discussion on the Richards Amendment which provided that half the military funds for Europe should be made available solely to the European Army, on its ratification: *Congressional Record – House*, 83rd Congress, 1st Session (1953), pp. 8689–93.
54 Statement by Dulles at a Press Conference at the Palais De Chaillot, 23 April 1953, as recorded in the *Congressional Record*, 83rd Congress, 1st Session, 1953, pp. 4853–4.
55 Dulles, at the Palais de Chaillot, 23 April 1953.

56 Joseph and Stewart Alsop, 'Matter of Fact – Plaster Jobs at Paris', in the *Washington Post*, 1 May 1953, recorded in the *Congressional Record*, 83rd Congress, 1st Session, 1953, pp. 4857–8.
57 Probably more out of propaganda for the domestic market than the religio-political fanaticism generally associated with him. See Coral Bell, *Negotiation From Strength*.
58 Eden, *Memoirs*, p. 99.
59 Eden, *Memoirs*, p. 64.
60 Eden, *Memoirs*, p. 63. See also, R. Goold-Adams, *The Time of Power: A Reappraisal of John Foster Dulles* (London 1962), p. 309.
61 See Drummond and Coblentz, *Duel at the Brink*, Chapter III, especially pp. 37–8.
62 Goold-Adams, *The Time of Power*, p. 309.
63 Goold-Adams, *The Time of Power*, p. 308.
64 Sen. J. W. Fulbright, 'Our Stake In A Federated Europe', recorded in the *Congressional Record*, 82nd Congress, 2nd Session (1952), p. 4874–6.
65 *The Times*, 21 January 1948.
66 Goold-Adams, *The Time of Power*, p. 309.
67 Conference of Strasbourg, November 1951, Debates, p. 49.
68 Dulles Papers: 'Estimate of the Situation', Folder: 1950.
69 J. F. Dulles, *War or Peace* (New York 1950), p. 160.
70 Goold-Adams, *The Time of Power*, p. 79.
71 For a comprehensive account of EDC see Daniel Lerner and Raymond Aron (ed.), *France Defeats EDC* (New York 1957).
72 Eisenhower, *The White House Years*, p. 400.
73 Eden, *Memoirs*, p. 58.
74 Eden, *Memoirs*, pp. 57–8. (My italics.) The implications of this statement are interesting, and it should be noted that members of the French Parliament and public had found reason to accuse Dulles of 'intolerable interference in internal French affairs', when he revealed his intentions of reappraising the fundamentals of American policy if France did not act 'soon' on EDC (Drummond and Coblentz, *Duel at the Brink*, p. 86).
75 Eden, *Memoirs*, p. 34.

Chapter 7

1 Dulles Papers: Department of State, Office Of The Secretary, September 1954. 1. Writings, G. Notes and Memoranda, 1950–9 Folder: 1954 (my italics).
2 Eden, *Memoirs*, p. 163.
3 Eden, *Memoirs*, p. 159.
4 Eisenhower, *The White House Years*, p. 404.
5 Eden, *Memoirs*, pp. 158–9.

6 Dulles Papers: *Item* C – Copy of memo of 27 April 1948, of secret
   meeting at Blair House between Secretary Marshall, Under-
   Secretary Lovett, Senator Vandenberg, and J. F. Dulles, with
   reference to the possible North Atlantic Treaty. 1. Writings,
   G. Notes and Memoranda, 1917–49, File: 1948.

7 Ibid.

8 Dulles Papers: Memorandum of Conversation between Secretary
   Acheson and Mr Dulles, 14 February 1949. 1. Writings, G. Notes
   and Memoranda, 1917–49, Folder: 1949.

9 Dulles Papers: Memorandum of Conversation between Secretary
   Acheson and Mr Dulles, 14 February 1949.

10 Eden, *Memoirs*, p. 163.

11 Eden, *Memoirs*, p. 163.

12 Eden, *Memoirs*, p. 163.

13 Eden, *Memoirs*, p. 163.

14 Eden, *Memoirs*, p. 164.

15 Eisenhower, *The White House Years*, p. 405.

16 Eisenhower, *The White House Years*, p. 406.

17 Eden, *Memoirs*, pp. 164–5.

18 Eden, *Memoirs*, p. 163.

19 Eden, *Memoirs*, p. 166.

20 The so-called Nine-Power Conference with representatives from the
   United States of America, and Canada, in addition to the five
   Brussels Pact members, the Federal Republic of Germany, and
   Italy.

21 The so-called Four Power Conference attended by the United States,
   France, the United Kingdom and the Federal Republic of Germany.

22 For details of the agreements reached at these meetings and of the
   Paris Agreements see, *NATO – Facts About The North Atlantic
   Treaty Organisation* – (NATO – Information Service – Paris,
   January 1962) Appendix 10, 'Documents Relating to the Accession
   to the Treaty of the Federal Republic of Germany – Paris Agree-
   ments, 23 October, 1954'.

23 Agreed to in the Bonn Agreement of 1952, which had depended on
   the ratification of EDC.

24 In the case of Britain, which had not been party to the EDC, it was
   four divisions and the Second Tactical Air Force; for Luxembourg,
   one regimental combat team. It should be noted that the maxima
   were understood in terms of 'equivalent fighting capacity'; and that
   the maxima did not represent a commitment to build up or maintain such forces, but indicated the right of the contracting parties so
   to do.

25 The main concern of the Agency was to control the peacetime arms
   levels agreed between the countries and to observe Germany's
   pledge not to develop atomic, chemical, or biological weapons.

L

26 The new statute was, however, rejected one year later, in October 1955, by the Saarlanders.
27 Eden, *Memoirs*, p. 165.
28 Excepting the necessary revision by Eden of going farther into Europe than the United States would go.
29 Memorandum for the Honorable James C. Hagerty, The White House – a copy of *The Report of Secretary of State Dulles to the Cabinet*, 25 October 1954, Eisenhower Papers, OF 101-P-2, pp. 7–8.
30 Dulles Cabinet Report, p. 8.
31 Eden, *Memoirs*, p. 168.
32 Dulles Cabinet Report, 25 October 1954, p. 11.
33 Eisenhower, *The White House Years*, p. 407.
34 Eisenhower, *The White House Years*, p. 409.
35 Eisenhower Papers: 'Text of the Message From the President to the Prime Ministers of the Seven Nations Signatory to the Protocols Establishing Western European Union. . .' 10 March 1955: Official File – 260-B.
36 Eisenhower Papers, 10 March 1955.
37 Eisenhower, *The White House Years*, p. 409.
38 Dulles Cabinet Report, 25 October 1954, pp. 11–12.
39 Dulles Cabinet Report, p. 16.
40 Dulles Cabinet Report, p. 18.
41 Dulles Cabinet Report, p. 21.
42 Dulles Cabinet Report, p. 10. (My italics.)

Epilogue

1 Bevin's speech, 22 January 1948. HC Debates, 5th Series, Vol. 446. CC. 398 ff.
2 Lord Strang, *Home and Abroad* (London 1956), p. 289.

Bibliography

PRIMARY SOURCES

Private Papers

William L. Clayton
(The Harry S. Truman Library, Independence, Missouri, USA)
Hugh Dalton
(The British Library of Political and Economic Science, London, England)
John Foster Dulles
(Princeton University Library, New Jersey, USA)
Dwight D. Eisenhower
(The Dwight D. Eisenhower Library, Abilene, Kansas, USA)
Ellen Clayton Garwood
(The Harry S. Truman Library, Independence, Missouri, USA)
Harry S. Truman
(The Harry S. Truman Library, Independence, Missouri, USA)

Official and Semi-Official Papers

Congressional Record, 80th, 81st, 82nd, 83rd Congresses (United States
    Government Printing Office, Washington DC, USA)
Parliamentary Debates: Hansard, 5th Series, Volumes 446, 450, 460, 477,
    495
Documents on American Foreign Relations, Volumes IX, X, XI, XII (by
    the World Peace Foundation to 1952, and then by the Council on
    Foreign Relations)
Documents on European Recovery and Defence, March 1947 – April 1949
    (London: Royal Institute of International Affairs, 1949)
Public Papers of the Presidents of the United States, Harry S. Truman (series
    of 6 volumes, 1945–1953) (Washington GPO)
*Conference of Strasbourg between delegations of the Congress of the United
    States of America and of the Consultative Assembly of the Council of
    Europe, Official Record of Debates, Strasbourg, November 19th–23rd,
    1951* (issued by the Secretariat-General of the Council of Europe)
Documents Relating To The Accession To The Treaty Of The Federal

Republic Of Germany – Paris Agreements, 23 October, 1954 (Appendix 10, in *NATO – Facts About The North Atlantic Treaty Organisation*, NATO Information Service, Paris, January 1962)

Extension of European Recovery, Hearings Before The Committee On Foreign Relations, United States Senate, Eighty-First Congress, First Session, on S.833, A Bill To Amend The Economic Cooperation Act of 1948, February 8, 9, 10, 11, 14, 15, 16, 17, and 28, 1949 (United States Government Printing Office, Washington, 1949)

Military Assistance Program, Joint Hearings Before The Committee On Foreign Relations And The Committee On Armed Services, United States Senate, Eighty-First Congress, First Session, on S.2388, A Bill To Promote The Foreign Policy And Provide For The Defense And General Welfare Of The United States By Furnishing Military Assistance To Foreign Nations, August 8, 9, 10, 11, 17, 18 and 19, 1949 (United States Government Printing Office, Washington, 1949)

Mutual Defense Assistance Program 1950–1951, Report Of The Committee On Foreign Relations And The Armed Services On S.3809, To Amend The Mutual Defence Assistance Act Of 1949; June 21, 1950, Eighty-First Congress, Second Session, Senate, Report No. 1853 (United States Government Printing Office, Washington, 1950)

The Mutual Security Act Of 1951, Report To Accompany H.R. 5113, August 27, 1951, Eighty-Second Congress, First Session, Senate, Report No. 703 (United States Government Printing Office, Washington)

The North Atlantic Treaty: Hearings Before The Committee On Foreign Relations, United States Senate, Eighty-First Congress, First Session, On Executive L, Eighty-First Congress, First Session, The North Atlantic Treaty – PART 1, Administration Witnesses, April 27, 28, 29, May 2, and 3, 1949 (United States Government Printing Office, Washington, 1949)

Ninth Report To Congress of the Economic Cooperation Administration, For the Quarter Ended June 30, 1950 (United States Government Printing Office, Washington)

Memoirs

ACHESON, DEAN G.
Present at The Creation (New York: W. W. Norton & Co. Inc., 1969)

ADENAUER, KONRAD
Konrad Adenauer, Memoirs 1945–1953 (English translation, London: Weidenfeld and Nicolson, 1966)

EDEN, ANTHONY
The Memoirs of the Rt. Hon. Sir Anthony Eden, K.G., P.C., M.C. – Full Circle (London: Cassell, 1960)

EISENHOWER, DWIGHT D.
The White House Years – Mandate For Change, 1953–1956 (London: Heinemann, 1963)

KENNAN, GEORGE F.
Memoirs, 1925–1950 (London: Hutchinson, 1968)
TRUMAN, H. S.
The Memoirs Of Harry S. Truman, Volume One – Year of Decisions, 1945 (London: Hodder and Stoughton, 1955)
The Memoirs Of Harry S. Truman, Volume Two – Years Of Trial And Hope, 1946–1953 (London: Hodder and Stoughton, 1956)

Interviews
Extensive interviews were held with:

Mr Dean G. Acheson
Washington DC, May 2, 1968
Ambassador W. Averell Harriman
Washington DC, April 30, 1968
Mr Paul G. Hoffman
New York, April 23, 1968
Professor George Kennan
Princeton, April 22, 1968

A number of other persons connected with the subject were also interviewed.

SECONDARY SOURCES

Selected Reading

ACHESON, DEAN G.
Sketches from Life of Men I have Known (New York: Harper and Row, 1961).
ADAMS, SHERMAN
Firsthand Report, The Story Of The Eisenhower Administration (New York: Harper and Row, 1961).
ALLEN, H. C.
Great Britain And The United States, A History of Anglo-American Relations (1783–1952) (London: Odhams, 1954).
BALL, GEORGE W.
The Discipline Of Power, Essentials Of A Modern World Structure (London: The Bodley Head Ltd., 1968).
BELL, CORAL
Negotiation From Strength, A Study In The Politics Of Power (London: Chatto & Windus, 1962).
The Debatable Alliance – An essay in Anglo-American relations (London: Oxford University Press, 1964).
BELOFF, MAX
The United States and the Unity of Europe (London: Faber, 1963).

BERDING, A. H.
Dulles On Diplomacy (Princeton, 1965).

CAMPS, MIRIAM
Britain And The European Community, 1955–1963 (London: Oxford University Press, 1965).
What Kind Of Europe? (London: Oxford University Press, 1965).

COUNCIL ON FOREIGN RELATIONS
Foreign Affairs Bibliography (1952–1962)
The United States in World Affairs (Annual Volumes), (New York: Harper and Row).

DIEBOLD, JR., WILLIAM C.
Trade and Payments in Western Europe, A Study in Economic Cooperation, 1947–1951 (New York: Harper, 1952).
The Schuman Plan, A Study in Economic Cooperation, 1950–1959 (New York: Praeger, 1959).

DRUMMOND, R. AND COBLENTZ, G.
Duel at the Brink (New York: Doubleday, 1960).

DULLES, J. F.
War or Peace (London: Harrap, 1950).

ELLIS, HOWARD S.
The Economists Of Freedom, The Progress and Future of Aid to Europe (New York: Harper and Row, 1950).

EPSTEIN, LEON, D.
Britain – Uneasy Ally (University of Chicago Press: 1954).

FORRESTAL, JAMES V.
The Forrestal Diaries (Walter Millis, ed.), (New York: Viking, 1951).

GARDNER, R. N.
Sterling-Dollar Diplomacy, Anglo-American Collaboration in The Reconstruction of Multilateral Trade (Oxford: The Clarendon Press, 1956).

GEIGER, THEODORE AND CLEVELAND, H. VAN BUREN
Making Western Europe Defensible (National Association, Planning Pamphlet 74, August 1951).

GOODWIN, GEOFFREY L.
Britain And The United Nations (London: Oxford University Press, 1957).

GOOLD-ADAMS, R.
The Time Of Power: A Reappraisal of John Foster Dulles (London: Weidenfeld and Nicolson, 1962).

HALLE, LOUIS J.
The Cold War as History (New York: Harper and Row, 1967).

HAVILAND, JR. H. FIELD (ED.)
The United States and the Western Community (Haverford, Pa., Haverford College Press, 1957).

HEISER, H. J.
British Policy with regard to the Unification Efforts on the European Continent (Leyden, Sythoff, 1959).

HERTER, CHRISTIAN
Toward an Atlantic Community (New York: Harper and Row, 1963).

ISMAY, HASTINGS L. (BARON)
NATO: The First Five Years, 1949–1954 (North Atlantic Treaty Organization: Utrecht, *imprint*, 1955).

JALÉE, PIERRE
The Pillage Of The Third World (Trans.) (New York: The Monthly Review, 1968).

JONES, JOSEPH M.
The Fifteen Weeks (New York: Viking, 1955).

KENNAN, GEORGE FROST
American Diplomacy, 1900–1950 (London: Secker and Warburg, 1952).

KIRKPATRICK, IVONE
The Inner Circle – Memoirs of Ivone Kirkpatrick (London, Macmillan, 1959).

KISSINGER, H. A.
The Necessity for Choice: prospects of American foreign policy (London: Chatto & Windus, 1960).
Nuclear Weapons and Foreign Policy (New York: Harper, 1957).

KRAFT, JOSEPH
The Grand Design (New York: Harper, 1962).

LABOUR PARTY
European Unity (London, 1950).

LERNER, DANIEL AND ARON, RAYMOND (EDS.)
France Defeats EDC (London: Thames & Hudson, 1957).

LILIENTHAL, DAVID
The Journals of David E. Lilienthal (Vol. II) The Atomic Energy Years (New York: Harper & Row, 1964).

LUARD, EVAN (ED.)
The Cold War: A Reappraisal (London: Thames & Hudson, 1964).

MALLALIEU, WILLIAM C.
British Reconstruction and American Policy, 1945–1955 (Mituchen, N. J.: Scarecrow Press Inc., 1956).

MAYNE, RICHARD
The Community of Europe (London: Gollancz. 1962).

MC INNIS, EDGAR
The Atlantic Triangle and the Cold War (Toronto: University of Toronto Press, 1959).

NICHOLAS, H. G.
Britain And The United States (London: Chatto and Windus, 1963).

NORTHEDGE, F. S.
British Foreign Policy – The Process of Readjustment, 1945–1961 (London: Allen and Unwin, 1962).

OSGOOD, R. E.
NATO, The Entangling Alliance (Chicago: University of Chicago Press, 1962).

PENROSE, E. F.
Economic Planning for the Peace (Princeton, N.J.: Princeton University Press, 1953).

PRICE, H. B.
The Marshall Plan and Its Meaning (New York: Cornell University Press, 1955).

ROBERTS, H. L. AND WILSON, P. A.
Britain and the United States, Problems in Cooperation (London: Royal Institute of International Affairs, 1953).

ROSTOW, W. W.
The United States in the World Arena (New York: Harper, 1960).

RUSSETT, BRUCE, M.
Community and Contention; Britain and America in the 20th Century (Cambridge, Mass.: Massachusetts Institute of Technology, 1963).

SPANIER, JOHN W.
American Foreign Policy Since World War II (New York: Praeger, 1960).

STRANG, W. (BARON)
Home and Abroad (London: André Deutsch, 1956).

UNITED STATES, DEPARTMENT OF STATE
Department of State Bulletin (Series 1949–1953) (Washington: US Department of State).

VANDENBERG, JR. ARTHUR H. AND MORRIS, J. A. (EDS.)
The Private Papers of Senator Vandenberg (Boston: Houghton Mifflin 1952).

WATT, D. C.
Personalities and Policies – Studies in The Formulation Of British Foreign Policy in the Twentieth Century (London: Longmans, 1965).

WILCOX, FRANCIS, O. AND HAVILAND, JR., H. FIELD (EDS.)
The Atlantic Community: Progress and Prospects (New York, Praeger, 1963).

WOLFERS, ARNOLD (ED.)
Alliance Policy in the Cold War (Baltimore, Johns Hopkins Press, 1959).

WOLFERS, ARNOLD
Discord and Collaboration: Essays on International Politics (Baltimore, Johns Hopkins Press, 1962).

Articles

BELOFF, MAX
'American Attitudes' (*The Atlantic Community Quarterly*, Vol. 1, No. 1, March 1963).

BOWIE, ROBERT
'Tensions Within The Alliance' (*Foreign Affairs*, October, 1953).

CONWAY, EDWARD A.

'Eisenhower And European Union' (*America, National Catholic Weekly*, issue of September 15, 1951, as printed in the *Congressional Record*, Appendix, 82nd Congress, 1st Session, pp. A5633-4).

CROMLEY, RAY

'Merger With United Kingdom' (*Wall Street Journal*, August 16, 1949, as printed in the *Congressional Record*, Appendix, 81st Congress, 1st Session, pp. A5348-9).

DAWSON, RAYMOND, AND ROSECRANCE, RICHARD

'Theory and Reality in the Anglo-American Alliance' (*World Politics, A Quarterly Journal of International Relations*, Vol. XIX, No. 1, October 1966).

FULBRIGHT, J. W.

'Our Stake in a Federated Europe' (*Maclean's Magazine*, March 1, 1948, as printed in the *Congressional Record*, Senate, 82nd Congress, 2nd Session, pp. 4874-6).

GELDER, LIONEL

'A Marriage Of Inconvenience' (*Foreign Affairs*, January, 1963).

GOLDBERG, ALFRED

'The Military Origins of the British Nuclear Deterrent' (*International Affairs*, October 1964).

GOTT, RICHARD

'The Evolution of the Independent British Deterrent' (*International Affairs*, April, 1963).

GROOM, A.

'The United States And The British Deterrent' (*London Institute Of World Affairs, Year Book*, 1964).

HALLE, LOUIS J.

'A Multitude Of Cold Wars' (*International Journal, Canadian Institute of International Affairs*, Vol. XXIII, No. 3, Summer 1968).

HOFFMAN, STANLEY

'The European Process At Atlantic Crosspurposes' (*Journal of Common Market Studies*, Vol. III, No. 2, February 1965).

KENNAN, GEORGE F.

'Mr. X' Articles (*Foreign Affairs*, July 1947 and April, 1951).

MALLALIEU, WILLIAM C.

'The Origin Of The Marshall Plan, A study in policy formation and national leadership' (*Political Science Quarterly*, Vol. LXXIII, Number 4, December, 1958).

RUML, BEARDSLEY

'The United States Of Europe: A Hope For Peace' (*Collier's Magazine*, June 21, 1952, as printed in the *Congressional Record*, Appendix, 82nd Congress, 2nd Session, p. A3849).

SAHM, ULRICH
'Britain And Europe, 1950' (*International Affairs*, Vol. 43, No. 1, January 1967).

Economist
'Britain In The Pillory' (*Economist*, August 13, 1949).
The World Today
'U.S. Bases in Britain' (*The World Today*, OUP, Vol. 60, No. 8, August 1960).

Index

Acheson, Dean, 11, 83; views on European unity, 14, 35; opposition to non-alignment, 28; British Labour Government and, 41, 58, 59, 60, 63; NATO and, 72, 73; Schuman Plan supported by, 87–8, 92; and EDC, 98–9, 102, 103; his view of Atlantic community, 105; accused of being 'fellow-traveller', 108; Anglo-American relationship supported by, 119–20

Adenauer, Konrad, 112; Franco-German *rapprochement* initiated by, 86–7; and Schuman Plan, 88; NATO and, 98; Dulles' close relationship with, 112, 114

Africa, 23, 52, 53

Agreed Declaration (1945: Anglo-American nuclear cooperation), 77

Agreement for Intra-European Payments and Compensation (1948), 42

Alsop, Joseph and Stewart, 112

Anglo-American Bases Agreement, 74

Anglo-American Financial Agreements (1945), 5, 18, 34, 39–40, 55

Anglo-French Treaty of Dunkirk (1947), 26

Anglo-Soviet Alliance (1942), 20

appeasement, 2–3, 108

Asia, 28, 53, 109

Asia-First Policy (of Dulles), 100–10, 111–12

Atlantic Charter (1941), 33

Atlantic Pact *see* NATO

Attlee, Clement, 9, 72, 78, 90–1

balance of payments, intra-European, 42, 46; British, 44, 49, 57–60; *see also* EPU

Belgium, 24, 43; overseas territories, 24, 53, 54, 130; intra-European trade, 43, 46; *see also* Benelux countries

Benelux countries, 115; Brussels Treaty, 26, 65; European integration favoured by, 29, 37, 63; Customs Union between, 38; London Programme and, 84; Schuman Plan accepted by, 88, 93; EDC and, 98, 116; Eden Plan supported by, 122; *see also* Belgium; Luxembourg; Netherlands

Berlin Blockade, 70, 84, 85

Berlin Crisis, 75

Bevin, Ernest, 38, 40, 97, 124, 127; policy toward European inter-governmental union of, vii–viii, 22; initiates ERP discussions, 9, 37; attitude to Soviet Union, 21; Western Union concept of, 22–6, 52, 55, 65, 89, 101, 130, 132; BTO created, 26, 65–6; and NATO, 26, 27, 67–8, 73; German policy, 83; opposition to Schuman Plan, 89, 91

Bidault, Georges, 9, 29

Boggs, US Representative, 13

Bonn Agreements (1951), 92

Bretton Woods (UN Monetary & Financial conference), 7, 34, 39

Britain, inter-governmental approach to European unity of, vii–viii, 21–2, 25, 29–30; Potsdam Conference and, 4–5; announces end of aid to Greece and Turkey, 6, 28; changing roles and conflicts within Anglo-American alliance, 16–31; post-war Soviet relations, 20–1; Bevin's Western Union policy, 22–6; BTO established, 26, 27, 65–6; military importance to USA of, 27–8; nuclear weapons research and development, 28, 78–80, 101; sterling crisis (1947), 34, 40–1; and devaluation (1949), 35, 57–60; intra-European trade liberalization, 43, 44–6; and increasing role of state trading, 46; opposition to EPU, 47–51; 1950 General Election, 50; opposition to German rearmament, 73; London Programme for reconstituting W. Germany, 83–6; EDC and, 97,